On Images, Visual Culture, Memory and the Play without a Script

READING AUGUSTINE

Series Editor:
Miles Hollingworth

Reading Augustine presents books that offer personal, nuanced and oftentimes literary readings of Saint Augustine of Hippo. Each time, the idea is to treat Augustine as a spiritual and intellectual icon of the Western tradition, and to read through him to some or other pressing concern of our current day, or to some enduring issue or theme. In this way, the writers follow the model of Augustine himself, who produced his famous output of words and ideas in active tussle with the world in which he lived. When the series launched, this approach could raise eyebrows, but now that technology and pandemics have brought us into the world and society like never before, and when scholarship is expected to live the same way and responsibly, the series is well-set and thriving.

Volumes in the series:

On Music, Sense, Affect, and Voice, Carol Harrison

On Solitude, Conscience, Love and Our Inner, and Outer Lives, Ron Haflidson

On Creation, Science, Disenchantment, and the Contours of Being and Knowing, Matthew W. Knotts

On Agamben, Arendt, Christianity, and the Dark Arts of Civilization, Peter Iver Kaufman

On Self-Harm, Narcissism, Atonement, and the Vulnerable Christ, David Vincent Meconi

On Faith, Works, Eternity, and the Creatures We Are, André Barbera

On Time, Change, History, and Conversion, Sean Hannan

On Compassion, Healing, Suffering, and the Purpose of the Emotional Life, Susan Wessel

On Consumer Culture, Identity, the Church and the Rhetorics of Delight, Mark Clavier

On Creativity, Liberty, Love and the Beauty of the Law, Todd Breyfogle

On Education, Formation, Citizenship and the Lost Purpose of Learning, Joseph Clair

On Ethics, Politics and Psychology in the Twenty-First Century, John Rist

On God, the Soul, Evil and the Rise of Christianity, John Peter Kenney

On Love, Confession, Surrender and the Moral Self, Ian Clausen

On Memory, Marriage, Tears, and Meditation, Margaret R. Miles

On Mystery, Ineffability, Silence, and Musical Symbolism, Laurence Wuidar

On Images, Visual Culture, Memory and the Play without a Script

Matthias Smalbrugge

t&tclark

LONDON • NEW YORK • OXFORD • NEW DELHI • SYDNEY

T&T CLARK
Bloomsbury Publishing Plc
50 Bedford Square, London, WC1B 3DP, UK
1385 Broadway, New York, NY 10018, USA
29 Earlsfort Terrace, Dublin 2, Ireland

BLOOMSBURY, T&T CLARK and the T&T Clark logo are trademarks of
Bloomsbury Publishing Plc

First published in Great Britain 2022

Copyright © Matthias Smalbrugge, 2022

Matthias Smalbrugge has asserted his right under the Copyright, Designs
and Patents Act, 1988, to be identified as Author of this work.

Cover image: Photo 12 / Alamy Stock Photo

All rights reserved. No part of this publication may be reproduced
or transmitted in any form or by any means, electronic or mechanical,
including photocopying, recording, or any information storage or retrieval
system, without prior permission in writing from the publishers.

Bloomsbury Publishing Inc does not have any control over,
or responsibility for, any third-party websites referred to or in this book.
All internet addresses given in this book were correct at the time of
going to press. The author and publisher regret any inconvenience
caused if addresses have changed or sites have ceased to exist, but
can accept no responsibility for any such changes.

A catalogue record for this book is available from the British Library.

Library of Congress Cataloging-in-Publication Data
Names: Smalbrugge, Matthias, author.
Title: On images, visual culture, memory and the play
without a script / Matthias Smalbrugge.
Description: London; New York: T&T Clark, 2021. | Series: Reading
Augustine | Includes bibliographical references and index. |
Identifiers: LCCN 2021015816 (print) | LCCN 2021015817 (ebook) | ISBN
9781501358845 (paperback) | ISBN 9781501358852 (hardback) | ISBN
9781501358869 (pdf) | ISBN 9781501358883 (epub).
Subjects: LCSH: Augustine, of Hippo, Saint, 354-430. | Image (Philosophy)
Classification: LCC B655.Z7 S63 2021 (print) |
LCC B655.Z7 (ebook) | DDC 189/.2–dc23
LC record available at https://lccn.loc.gov/2021015816
LC ebook record available at https://lccn.loc.gov/2021015817

ISBN: HB: 978-1-5013-5885-2
PB: 978-1-5013-5884-5
ePDF: 978-1-5013-5886-9
ePUB: 978-1-5013-5888-3

Series: Reading Augustine

Typeset by Integra Software Services Pvt. Ltd.

To find out more about our authors and books visit www.bloomsbury.com and
sign up for our newsletters.

CONTENTS

Overview ix
Abbreviations xi

1 Introduction: The cultural predominance of the image and its multilayered nature 1
   The first narrative on image: Echo and Narcissus 5
   The second narrative on image: The selfie 11
   The third narrative on image: The autobiography 14
   Concluding remarks about narratives and images 18

2 The image as a shadow: Plato's cave 21
   The shadow: A particular image 24
   The moral problem: What is the image an image of? 27
   The return of the Philosopher 33

3 Augustine and the broader focus on image 37
   The platonic background 39
   The main aspects of image: Similarity and dissimilarity 45
   Similarity and participation 51
   God as similarity itself: The Trinity and human dissimilarity 53
   About sin 59

4 The different forms of similarity 69
   The Augustinian ambivalence 74
   Another approach to dissimilarity and of moral failure 78
   The ultimate ambivalence: Love and contempt 84
   A second ambivalence: Who is who in our memory? 86

CONTENTS

5 *De Trinitate* 93
   Some general remarks on *De Trinitate* 94
   Love and knowledge 104
   The image as the cradle of love and knowledge 107
   The double nature of images due to the will 112
   The image turning to itself: The perversion of
   self-reference 116
   The image turning to itself: More than perversion 120

6 The final question: It's all about language 129
   The loss of language 132
   Echo revisited 138
   Conclusion 141

Bibliography 150
Index 158

OVERVIEW

In this essay, the author attempts to discover some structures that have determined our current position when it comes to image. The notion of image itself has many meanings. We can speak about image as the reflection of a certain reality, about image as a sculpture, about image as the way I craft my own identity and so on. All these notions of image have something in common: they refer, normally speaking, to a reality that lies behind the image. Behind the sculpture there is an original behind my image, there is a story, an identity. At least, so it was. In modern times, this connection seems to be increasingly fragile. Images no longer need a 'background'; they act as realities that are no longer bound to any underlying structure. It is, for example, possible to create images that are no longer based on facts but that suggest alternative facts. It is possible to create images that have nothing to do with our need to understand, but rather with our longing for a one-dimensional truth that suits us.

In order to understand this modern use of image, this book analyses as its main thesis the Augustinian concept of image, concluding that Augustine created an ambivalence regarding the image that could not be overcome within the history of a mainly Christian culture. On the one hand, according to Augustine, the image was a God-given present, implying humans were capable of behaving and acting in a godlike manner. That was the constructive side of the Augustinian image. On the other hand, Augustine made clear that this image was spoiled and no longer capable, due to the Fall, to be a constructive element in human lives. This imbalance between construction and destruction was to remain the main frame of our culture when it came to image. This book tries to analyse how Augustine constructed this disbalance, how he tried to solve it and how, unfortunately, he chose the option of deconstruction. This also implies that he made it difficult for humans to act in a morally acceptable way.

The book starts with some examples of images, namely the myth of Echo and Narcissus, the selfie and the autobiography. It then continues with an analysis of Plato's cave and moves on to the works of Augustine. It first deals with the *Soliloquies*, where the notions of similarity and dissimilarity are introduced. These notions will be the chorus line of the Augustinian approach of the image. Having studied these notions more in detail, the book moves on to Augustine's book on the Trinity and tries to understand the final choices Augustine made concerning images. The conclusion then is that the Bishop of Hippo indeed left us with a spiritual heritage that was highly unbalanced. Nevertheless, he also left us some models that could be considered an antidote against his own deconstruction.

ABBREVIATIONS

Augustine's works

Confessiones	Conf.
Contra Duas Epistolas Pleagianorum	C Duas Ep. Pel.
Contra Faustum	Contra Faustum
De Beata Vita	De Beata Vita
De Ciuitate Dei	De Ciu.
De Diuersis Quaestionibus LXXXXIII	De Diu. Q. LXXXIII
De Doctrina Christiana	De Doct. Chr.
De Genesi ad Litteram Libri Duodecim	De Gen. ad Litt.
De Genesi ad Litteram Liber Imperfectus	De Gen. Imp.
De Genesi contra Manichaeos	De Genesi contra Man.
De Libero Arbitrio	De Lib. Arb.
De Magistro	De Mag.
De Trinitate	De Trin.
De Vera Religione	De Vera Rel.
Soliloquia	Sol.

Classical authors

Plato: *Politeia*	Pol.
Plotinus: *Enneades*	Enn.

1

Introduction: The cultural predominance of the image and its multilayered nature

Imagine! Pronounce this simple word and the effect on your interlocutor will be surprising. First, he will be eager to know what he must imagine. Although he does not know what he will have to imagine, his imagination will already be ahead of his thinking, imagining what he should possibly have to image. Then, once you have continued and said 'Imagine a car', this imagined car will cause an explosion of cars: small ones, red ones, modern ones and second-hand ones. We will not dwell any further on cars, but the word 'imagine' has many layers we are hardly aware of. It is on these layers that we will focus first. Let us imagine ourselves watching an election debate on television. Looking at our screen, we watch politicians discussing problems as well as the solutions they will apply once they are elected. Looking at them, we try to determine their underlying vision and how they might act, negotiate and compromise in the near future. We listen attentively because what they discuss is nothing else than *our* world, *our* society and *our* lives. At the same time, however, it is of course no less *their* world and *their* society. In fact, these politicians are speaking about our common world, the reality we share. We hear them constructing and reconstructing this common reality as if reality is something one could change and mould as one could wax models, something that must befit one's expectations. What we are watching, therefore, is a huge and endless construction, deconstruction and reconstruction of our common reality. It is an avalanche of images,[1] only because a journalist asks about, for instance the National Health Service (NHS). This comes down to evoking the inner structure of 'imagine'.

Yet there is more to our common reality than this construction and reconstruction. Admittedly, the politicians we are looking at seek to picture the actual reality as well as the future one they intend to realize, using various images. However, it is not only the outside world of which they speak. They are also speaking about themselves, even if it is not done explicitly, evoking once again a reality that is composed of images. Is it not true that when one speaks about the future society one wants to construct, one also speaks of the man who will realize it all? Indeed, one speaks about oneself. Therefore, we also hear these politicians constructing images of themselves, what they want to be and what they will be once they have entered office and are in charge. However, both elements – the image of what they currently are and the image of what they want to be – are images destined to show us how they want to be seen by the public.[2]

---

[1] A very rich introduction to the theme of images and their use has been published by David Freedberg, *The Power of Images: Studies in the History and Theory of Response*, Chicago/London 1989. It is an overlook of the cultural use of images, and in particular the way we react on images. It has the great merit of showing that images are never emotionally speaking neutral. We do respond to them in an emotional way, independently whether we are speaking about 'higher' or 'lower' culture.

[2] The public and intentional use of portraits and sculptures is well known in cultural history. The Greeks and Romans already used portraits for 'propaganda' objectives and the same goes for the French monarchy. Both are fascinating examples of how to deal with the image of one self in the public sphere. Cp. Jane Fejfer, 'Selves and Others: Ways of Expressing Identity in the Roman Male Portrait', in *Roman Portraits in Context*, Berlin, New York 2008, 262–327, and Ronit Milano, 'The Face of the Monarchy: Court Propaganda and the Portrait Bust', in *The Portrait Bust and French Cultural Politics in the Eighteenth Century*, Leiden/Boston 2015, who describes in detail how the French monarchy struggled with different expectations of fatherhood, masculinity, divine office, fatherly love. The analysis of the portrait of Louis XIV by Bernini emphasizes that this portrait is already an answer to the upcoming 'public opinion' and the need to create images, satisfying this newborn public opinion. See also the beautiful and famous study of Peter Burke, *The Fabrication of Louis XIV*, New Haven 1992.

What we are looking at is politicians practising self-fashioning in order to achieve certain goals.[3] The images they present are not meant to give us a precise rendering of reality; on the contrary, they only represent certain pictures of reality, allowing us to 'model' our world and present it as a flexible one. These images, therefore, are meant to meet certain expectations, convictions, hopes and fears. Hence, although we were aware of it unconsciously, we come to realize that the so-called actual reality these politicians are speaking of is not something objective, something that exists outside them, but rather a multitude of concepts, flexible images, created according to a specific goal. Likewise, this 'imaginary' world in turn produces new images, produced by the first images evoked. An image may seem an enchanting one and new images will easily come forth. It may also be a frightening image, yet it will produce no fewer new images. Many reactions are possible and, depending on whether we feel aroused, attracted or disgusted by the images conjured, different ones will follow. Images thus act as instruments used to bridge the gap between language, thinking and reality.[4] They allow us to express our thoughts without moulding them too strictly into a pattern of words and phrases. They allow our thoughts to look for the right words. A perfect example of such flexibility is *Exercices de style* by Raymond Queneau,[5] in which the author pictures a man he met in a bus in Paris. Depending on whether the author considers this an aristocrat or a parvenu, images will pop up that will produce other images. In the end, there will be ninety-nine stories of this incidental meeting where words create images and images create words. Thus, in the case of the politicians, the visual elements of a

---

[3]Stephen Greenblatt, *Renaissance Self-Fashioning: From More to Shakespeare*, Chicago 2005. Greenblatt is the author who introduced the notion of self-fashioning as a way to understand literary products. Self-fashioning is most of all needed in circumstances where the actor moves from one public to the other and where he must change his outlook with regard to his audience. His concept of self-fashioning, already dating from 1980, became one of the most compelling frames of interpretation of literature. Greenblatt based himself on Foucault, who had shown how societal structures create the individual personality. See also, Stephen Greenblatt, Catherine Gallagher, *Practising New Historicism*, Chicago 2000.
[4]John A. Bateman, *Text and Image, a Critical Introduction to the Visual-Verbal Divide*, London 2014.
[5]Raymond Queneau, *Exercices de style*, Paris 1982.

broadcast programme perfectly reflect the images evoked by words. Look at this politician, hear him speak and realize that the images he uses can make the difference. Either we believe him, or we do not.[6] We believe him because of the strength of certain images – nothing less, nothing more.

What we discover is a world that seemingly only exists of images – images of politicians and images of the world that surrounds us – and we might even wonder whether there exists something we could call reality. Alternatively, is there only the image, a performative reality, a performative identity? Imagine if there were only images. Would there be anything behind them, and where would the series of images stop? When I imagine images, I imagine myself imaging images, and so on; yet the chain cannot be infinite. Logically speaking, an image must be the image of something that is not an image. Otherwise, the image would become the original and it would represent, at an ontological level, a very different being. The image, to remain an image at an ontological level, must obey its nature; that is, it must reflect a reality. This reality, however, is not graspable without it being caught in images that allow us to make such a reality visible, understandable and manageable. It is the image that points at the reality and that allows us to speak of it. There is no reality without images, and therefore, images can be considered the cultural structures we use to reveal what we call 'reality'. These images may be dreams, visions, political programmes, nightmares, fears and hopes; they are the elements that allow us to look at ourselves, the outer world, our neighbours, our society, our past and our present. Yet as cultural structures, they are paradoxical. They are not reality; however, to get in touch with reality, we cannot do without them. They must be considered the narrative structures we use to understand the world around us.

Now, what interests me is the image as a concept, a cultural structure we meet in different settings. The narratives, in the widest sense of the word, that we use. This book, therefore, intends to concentrate on the images we create of our lives, of our convictions, beliefs, loves and professions. I do so by focusing

---

[6]Mary E. Hocks, Michelle R. Kendrick eds. *Eloquent Images: Words and Images in the Age of New Media*, Cambridge, MA 2003.

mainly on St Augustine, who developed a theory of image, although this theory functions itself as an image and a multilayered one. What struck me most is that image is perhaps no longer an element pointing at the reality and henceforth referential;[7] perhaps today it rather refers to itself, and the classical distinction at the ontological level between image and original seems to have been abandoned. However, this can only be, at this very early stage of the book, a hypothesis, and to make it plausible, much work remains to be done. Suffice it to think, at a conceptual level, of the analysis of narrative structures such as *mimesis, imitation, reflection* and *representation*.[8] Therefore, I first attempt to analyse in more detail the multilayered nature of the image. Next, I turn to Plato and his idea on images and then the main part of this book deals with the Augustinian concept of image. Finally, the conclusion brings us back to modern times.

The first narrative on image: Echo and Narcissus

This time, imagine yourself not watching a debate on television but taking a selfie. No type of photo is popular in our era as the selfie. Since smartphones offer these possibilities of portraying ourselves, we seem to be irresistibly attracted by this continuous mirroring of ourselves. This mirroring offers the possibility not only to have a real mirror in front of you but also to keep the image for as long as you want. A traditional mirror loses the image it reflects once the person in front of it has stepped away, and this has definitely changed. The 'mirror' can preserve the image a person was just looking at, and this image can even be 'corrected' in the sense one wants to adjust it. The selfie, once it has been photoshopped, is like a mirror storing your image even if you are no longer in front of it. Finally, a possibility exists to keep the ideal image in the mirror and to love it – love it until

---

[7] Cp. Michel Melot, 'L'image n'est plus ce qu'elle était', *Revue documentaliste, Sciences de l'Information* 42 (2005/6) 361–5.
[8] Cp. John D. Lyons, Stephen G. Nichols Jr. eds., *Mimesis: From Mirror to Method, Augustine to Descartes*, Hanover/London 1982.

the next selfie shows you even a better image. Moreover, this image is one you can show to others, and hence, it is a short story about yourself. What, then, is this story you are telling about yourself? How do you relate to the image you pictured?

This question is magnificently treated in the myth of Echo and Narcissus, related by Ovid in his *Metamorphoses*,[9] though one might perhaps not immediately link this myth to the question of images and selfies.[10] However, upon closer examination, we can see that Echo ultimately became nothing less than the eternal image of Narcissus, and perhaps also the inverse, implying that they mirror each other. The story is a well-known one: Echo is a nymph who was punished by Hera for covering up the escapades of Zeus.[11] She is no longer capable of speaking like all other human and divine creatures; she can only repeat what she has heard – and even that only imperfectly; that is, she can only repeat the last words of what was said. Alas, she falls in love with Narcissus, a beautiful young man who is only interested in hunting. He is totally uninterested in women and even feels frightened by them. Therefore, once he becomes aware of Echo's love for him, his only desire is to flee, to flee as far and as soon as he can; however, the more Narcissus flees, the more Echo follows him and the more frightened he becomes. Once Echo becomes aware of the fact that he does not love her and that he constantly flees from her, she becomes a cry of despair, an emptied body, petrified, still only capable of repeating what she hears. Indeed, at the very moment that Narcissus cries out to his comrades 'let's go together', she repeats the last word 'together', defining exactly what an image is: a reflection of an original that has no means to exist individually. The original and

---

[9] Ovid, *Metamorphoses* III, 339–510.
[10] The relation between selfies and the myth of Echo and Narcissus has struck more than one researcher. Cp. Seunga Venus Jin and Ehri Ryu, '"The Paradox of Narcissus and Echo in the Instagram Pond" in Light of the Selfie Culture from Freudian Evolutionary Psychology: Self-Loving and Confident but Lonely', *Journal of Broadcasting & Electronic Media* 62 (2018) 554–77. Daniel Halpert, Sebastián Valenzuela, 'Selfie-ists or "Narci-selfiers"?: A Cross-Lagged Panel Analysis of Selfie Taking and Narcissism', *Personality and Individual Differences* 97 (2016) 98–101. These studies however are largely focused on the concept of narcissism and do not deal with the issue of image as such.
[11] I use the Greek names as they are better known than the Latin ones.

image, they must 'go together'.[12] At the same time, being capable of only repeating what she has heard imperfectly, Echo shows that the image is not a kind of perfect reflection of reality, but rather that it has its own dynamics and structure. For example, there is a gender aspect that strikes the reader. We are looking at a woman repeating the mere words of a man and being completely dependent on what he says. Indeed, Echo is completely dependent, but this striking dependency does not impede her from reflecting a gender that is the opposite of her own. Therefore, what she reveals is that identity is something fluent, though at the same time bound by fixed structures. On the one hand, she is capable of reflecting the opposite gender, whereas on the other hand, she must stick to his words. Indeed, original and image go together, but although they create a certain identity, this will always be a different one. Image and original create a performative identity. This might be characterized as a positive element in the story, yet there is also a less positive element. Echo also reveals that an image can become something void, a void that is not only created by the dependency already noticed, but also by the absence of a living relationship that must exist between the original and the image. Otherwise, the image becomes a petrified element that can only serve as a fixed identity with some essentialist traits. Hence, it is clear that there is also a destructive element in the relationship between reality and image. In other words, because Echo's only desire consists of cleaving to Narcissus, she loses the flexible character of her own identity and ends up as a mere petrified echo of her beloved one.

There is yet more to be attentive to. Narcissus from his side rejects Echo without any hesitation. It is fear that drives him without knowing what this fear is about. Yet one might reasonably suppose it is the fear of being captured and swallowed by Echo, who can only imperfectly reflect his being. It is the mere symbiosis he fears, as he does not want to be identified with an image that in no way reinforces his identity but only weakens it. Certainly, it is not identification in itself he rejects – he would love such a symbiosis, but only if the image he is looking for increases his self-confidence. This implies that he is fleeing reality and only looking for some sort

---

[12]Ovid, *Metamorposes* III, 386, *'huc coeamus' ait, nullique libentius umquam responsura sono 'coeamus' rettulit Echo.*

of ideal that never will come true. Echo represents, so to speak, the reality principle confronting Narcissus with the scattered structure of a real identity. That, however, is very far from what Narcissus longs for. What he is longing for is the ideal image of himself: an image that would be nothing else than repetition and that could be completely identified with the original, thus enhancing the original. In that case, however, is there still an image? Or is this particular longing a longing for an original that is deeply unsatisfied, and that therefore only strives towards an image that would calm its fear by showing a more or less perfect image? If that were true, Narcissus would be characterized by a desire that does not speak its name nor reveal its depth, but that might indeed swallow him. He could be drowning in this unknown desire. In the end, this is what happens to Narcissus, but we are not yet there. Now, having escaped from Echo, he rests beside a pond and suddenly discovers a beautiful image in the pond looking back at him. The effect is an astonishing one: he falls in love with the image. However, when he reaches out to touch this miraculous image, it vanishes as soon as he touches the water. He does not understand what is happening. The beloved one also seems in love with him, as is clearly shown by his gestures and movements. If Narcissus stretches out his arms, the other repeats the movements exactly. Yet although he also seems to be in love with Narcissus, he flees at the moment of embrace. Once the water is touched, he is gone. He echoes all Narcissus does, but this time the roles are reversed. It is no longer Narcissus who flees, but rather this enigmatic image, this unseizable second Echo. Unexpectedly, the author warns him against the fallacy of the image: '*Why are you trying to capture fugitive reflections? These are only shadows of an image that reflects; it has nothing of itself, it comes with you and stays with you.*'[13] Notwithstanding this warning, Narcissus only slowly comes to realize, in the confrontation with his own image, that he has fallen in love with himself and, to a certain extent, he did not know who he was.[14] Now, though, he does; he realizes that he is looking at an image of himself, but unfortunately he cannot

---

[13]*Metamorphoses* III, 432, *credule, quid frustra simulacra fugacia captas? quod petis, est nusquam; quod amas, avertere, perdes! Ista repercussae, quam cernis, imaginis umbra est: nil habet ista sui; tecum venitque manetque;*

[14]Which is exactly according to the prediction of Teiresias, that Narcissus would live on as long as he does not know himself (III, 348).

reach himself. This is despite his image being nothing less than the exact reflection of the original, which frightens him, because his image cannot deceive him: *nec me mea fallit imago*.[15] He realizes that the image is indeed an image and not the original, but where then is the original if there is no difference between the image and that of which it is the image? He obviously senses that his identity lies in this image, and he thus places his identity outside himself. Or perhaps he rather strives to unify the image with the original, something that is impossible because the seer and that which is seen, subject and object, can never be unified. This being the case and being obliged to long for an image he can never reach, he ends up like Echo, who lost her bodily existence and remained only a dwindling voice.[16] Narcissus also loses his corporeal existence;[17] he drowns in his desire and his body is consumed by the love of his image.

Therefore, what is emphasized in this beautiful story is the difficult relation between me and myself,[18] between me and the other, which simultaneously allows me to become myself and to obtain an identity.[19] However, it is also a story about desire and

---

[15] *Metamorphoses* III, 364, *iste ego sum: sensi, nec me mea fallit imago*.

[16] *Metamorphoses* III, 399, *vox manet, ossa ferunt lapidis traxisse figuram*.

[17] *Metamorphoses* III, 493, *nec corpus remanet, quondam quod amaverat Echo*.

[18] Compare the striking parallel with Augustine's writing in the *Confessions*. He is very much aware of this incomprehensible relation between image and reality and illustrates it by comparing ourselves to our dreaming selves. What in fact is the difference between the dreamer and the one who recalls the dream once the dream is dreamt. Is there a difference or should we say that the dreamer and the one who recalls his dreams are of course identical? Or perhaps quite different? As he puts it in *Conf.* X,30,41: what is the difference between me and myself? The only author to my knowledge who has seen a parallel between Augustine's work and the myth of Narcissus is Fr. David Vincent Meconi, 'Ravishing Ruin: Self-Loathing in Saint Augustine', *Augustinian Studies* 45 (2014) 227–46. However, on a possible narcissistic character of Augustine's writings, many authors have expanded in detail. See for an overview Paul Rigby, *Was Augustine a Narcissist?* Augustinian Studies 44 (2013) 59–91.

[19] Lisa Folkmarson Käll, 'A Voice of Her own: Echo's Own Echo', *Continental Philosophy Review* 48 (2015) 59–75. The interesting thing is that Käll considers Echo's words not purely as an echo but also as an original. Which complicates of course the relation between original and image, but it also makes clear that there is no definite presence of the original without an 'original' image of this original. As Narcissus exclaims himself: *iste ego sum* (III, 463). See also, Ingo Gildenhard, Andrew Zissos, 'Ovid's Narcissus (Met. 3,39–510): Echoes of Oedipus', *The American Journal of Philosophy* 121 (2000) 129–47.

fear. Most of all, it is a story about knowledge and its dynamics. What Echo expresses is the profound wish to be more than just a reflective mode of being, a kind of *mimesis* that remains an eternal process of repeating someone else's words, deeds, acts and so on. Her ideal, one might say, is to be an image that is different from the original, yet one that longs to be united with it. It is the idea that the image and the original need each other, even though they are quite different, because there is no other way to achieve knowledge. Why? Because knowledge means identifying oneself with an object without wiping out the boundaries. Indeed, an original cannot exist without an image and vice versa, very much like how a subject cannot exist without an object. Echo, in that sense, represents the ideal of a scholar, of an artist, who wants to 'touch' and 'identify' his or her object without being able to do so. There is always a horizon one cannot reach. The heart of knowledge will never be accessible and in the quest for this heart, one will always be a lonely hunter, much like Echo. That is why, although tragic, this ideal of knowledge remains the very positive aspect of the image. It shows us the desire for an almost symbiotic love, which is a desire that can never be fulfilled and that is nothing less than a bottomless pit. One can easily drown in such a desire. Yet at the same time, the fear exists of being nothing more than a repetition of someone else's words, that is, vain knowledge. Hence, it is due to its constantly changing nature that knowledge increases, changes and will always cross traditional boundaries. That is the multisided nature of Echo. Now, unexpectedly, these are also the aspects we come across in Ovid's picture of Narcissus. This time, however, it is not the image longing for the original (Echo's desire for Narcissus), but rather the opposite, namely the original wanting to join the image. Narcissus is misled by Echo's voice, but nevertheless cries out 'come here and let's go together'.[20] However, once Echo obeys and comes nearer, Narcissus immediately flies and shouts at her 'take away these arms that want to embrace'.[21] Again, Echo has no choice but to obey and to stay behind. She was invited to come close and then was rejected, which is the paradox that ruins her life. There is no possibility to

---

[20]*Metamorphoses* III,385: *alternae deceptus imagine vocis 'huc coeamus' ait, nullique libentius umquam responsura sono 'coeamus' rettulit Echo.*
[21]*Ibid.: Manus complexibus aufer.*

be a real image and to be valued as such. Knowledge will always be partial and imperfect. On the other hand, Narcissus does represent a certain ideal. There is of course the narcissistic tendency to only admire one's own image, but Narcissus is more than this traditional typology belonging to the psychiatric manual – he is not a one-dimensional type. As is rightly observed by Greg Stone,[22] Narcissus is no less than Echo, the one who longs for real knowledge in the most absolute sense of the word, where knowledge becomes beauty in the purest sense of the word, the ideal identification of subject and object. In that sense, argues Stone, he has the same desire as Echo and he can also be seen to represent an artist, a painter, wanting to realize a portrait that perfectly reflects the original. That is the way Caravaggio and Nicolas Poussin painted Narcissus, as the artist looking into the pond to find the ideal composition. This way of interpreting the myth also seems an acceptable one, but then again, the tragic aspect is unavoidable. This time it is not the original that suffers from a paradoxical nature, it is the image. It repeats the original, even in a perfect way, but refuses to be touched. Narcissus eagerly longs to join his image, but he will never be able to do so and therefore dies from his desire. He plunges into the water to embrace his image, but it is like the knife of Dorian Gray stabbing the blade into his own image. Once again, perfect knowledge seems to be out of reach. The conclusion is a simple one: knowledge is a composition of original and image, who, each in their turn, long for each other. Yet they cannot reach one another. If, however, these dynamics were to be abolished and this mutual longing were to no longer exist, real knowledge and real love would lose the truth that belongs to them, as is the case with Echo and Narcissus.

The second narrative on image: The selfie

Let us return to the selfie. If we look at Narcissus and Echo, what then is a selfie? Is it my longing for myself, the quest for knowledge

---

[22]Greg Stone, 'The Myth of Narcissus as a Surreptitious Allegory about Creativity', *Philosophy and Literature* 40 (2016) 273–84.

and beauty? Am I Narcissus when I take a selfie? Or am I trying to 'repeat' myself in a picture, longing to identify myself with a more perfect ideal, just as Echo did? The selfie at least seems to represent the irresistible attraction which these pictures of ourselves exert on us, albeit with a mixture of desire and fear. We are incomprehensibly drawn to the image, apparently because it is the best way to exist: we have to go together. Yet, is it love that drives us to the image, the love for beauty and knowledge? Or do we flee it once it does not satisfy our amour-propre? Is our frequent photoshopping compatible with the real sense of beauty? Or is it our incapacity to cope with our imperfections, just as fashion can either be a way to cope with one's imperfections or a manner to express a desire for real beauty? Hence, for example, the fierce debates on the 'photoshopping' that fashion can also represent, and the image it imposes on women.[23] Does fashion, therefore, reduce us to mere Echoes? This, in any case, is the risk involved in the selfie, and the same goes for Facebook. I might prefer my image, the selfie, to my ordinary personal reality, at least as I imagine it. Can we then consider the selfie as a self-portrait? Certainly, although not in the classical term.[24] We are not dealing with the 'official' self-portraiture, a picture hanging in a museum, where the painted eyes are looking at us, asking us at whom we are looking: the painter, his image or ourselves? A selfie is obviously not charged with all these questions, at least at first glance. It is taken in a wink, considered acceptable or not, and, according to this judgement, either stored and conserved or thrown away in the electronic bin. It has beauty, flattery or fun as criteria, which is not the case in classically painted self-portraits.[25] This makes us aware of the fact that a selfie is perhaps one single moment among the many, many moments we live. There is a longing to boost oneself; for example, if I want to create a visible memory of my visit to a beautiful city, to say hello to my loved ones far away, or to show that I am self-confident. I take a selfie and put it directly on Facebook. All these elements make the selfie a multilayered image. It has the

---

[23] The most famous of these criticisms is undoubtedly Naomi Wolf, *The Beauty Myth: How Images of Beauty Are Used against Women*, New York 1990/2002.
[24] James Hall, *The Self-Portrait: A Cultural History*, London 2014.
[25] Cp. Ernst van De Wetering, ed., *A Corpus of Rembrandt Paintings: The Self-Portraits*, New York 2005. The authors insist on the economic pressure leading to the production of self-portraits.

positive aspects of the image, but no less the negative ones, and we do not know which one prevails. It is a kind of short story. Perhaps it is even the shortest short story we have. Yet it has many possible interpretations, both constructive and destructive. Of course it can be a story about the need to boost oneself, but it can also be a story about the distance between the image I love and the self I hate, for I am not, alas, the one I want to be. Thanks to the selfie, I can destroy the reality behind it because I do not accept a reality different from the beautiful image I created. Indeed, the selfie is therefore constructive and destructive. That, at least, is something we might discover in this passing moment: an image can build or destroy and, as a short story, it can be constructive or destructive. A selfie could be a moment of self-reflection: who am I? Am I this very image or is the reality of my existence larger than the image? Whatever it may be, the risk is obvious: the image tends to become the standard we have to live up to, which in fact would inverse the normal ontological order. It is not the image referring to a reality behind it; it is an image that is meant to serve as a model for reality. It is the ultimate dream of Narcissus: looking at the image of oneself and trying to unify with it in a new reality. My personal reality does not matter anymore; it is just the rough material allowing me to create a new reality – although this new reality is only accessible within the small dimensions of a picture frame. However, it is also a play with the notions of reality and image. Both have to go together but neither of them can claim to be the starting point or to be the 'truth'. Both are flexible forms of being we can model according to our wishes. The selfie is also this infinite play with reality; it is the ultimate consequence of arguing that what exists, exists only in the eye of the beholder. In this sense, it is a late echo of Berkeley's *esse est percipi* (reality is what is seen) and it can be a very exciting exercise for creating a new relationship between reality and image. It is not only a proof of a kind of new form of vanity, of narcissism, but also what art constantly tries to do: it refines and reshapes the relationship between reality and image. Let us conclude; the selfie is a modern philosophical question about personal existence and the way one can or cannot preserve individuality by imagining it. It has a constructive and destructive aspect in it, and therefore, is a question about the relation between image and reality and vice versa. Moreover, it tends to inverse the order between image and reality, the latter now being constructed according to the demands of the image. However, in that sense, it is almost a form of art – it is creativity instead of narcissism. Hence, focusing on the relationship between image and reality, it is a question about knowing. In brief, the issue of the selfie is perhaps not about the perfect image, but rather about the perfect knowledge. Perfect knowledge in turn can be a deep longing, an extremely strong desire.

The third narrative on image: The autobiography

This brings us definitively to stories that symbolize this quest for knowledge. Not knowledge in a general sense, but rather knowledge that deals specifically with the relationship between image and reality, especially my personal reality. This is what autobiographies deal with. A selfie, indeed, is a short story about me and myself, a short philosophical project. An autobiography, by contrast, is much more than a short story. It is not a moment; it is the image of myself slowly constructed by time. It is a detailed story – becoming history – in which the author consciously deals with several aspects of him/herself during a great many years. Yet here again, as a narrative, it also has a complicated relationship with reality. The reality it focuses on is the author, but this reality is constantly changing. Furthermore, the fact of writing about oneself is to change oneself. It is already a first step towards the reversal of the relationship between reality and image, the image now creating its own reality. Therefore, in a certain manner, the autobiography shows us ways of self-fashioning, in which neither the original nor the image can be properly distinguished. Is there, in the case of the autobiography, still room for the distinction between original and image? Or is the image already imposing its own reality?

One of the best examples of this dilemma is of course Augustine, the author of *Confessions*, considered the first autobiography, although he also wrote other works containing autobiographical elements.[26] In the case of *Confessions*, the term 'autobiography'

---

[26] Cp. Matthias Smalbrugge, 'Augustine's Reception of Augustine: How to Write History, How to Compare Images', *Sacris Erudiri* 58 (2019) 145–70.

may be erroneous,[27] but Augustine certainly paid much attention to the aspect of 'auto-fiction', fashioning his life according to his own choices. So where can we find, if at all, the distinction between original and image in his work? This question is far from easy. What he did, in fact, was to create a new genre, and he did so by basing himself both on classical examples of this kind of literature[28] as well as on Christian ones – if ever these two elements can be distinguished.[29] Though perhaps not comparable to a modern autobiography, the publication of *Confessions* was in a way indeed the very moment of the birth of a new genre, and it was an important moment. It is the very moment an author consciously decided to picture himself and to publish it! Augustine called the work *Confessions* because this word already contains several layers, ranging from confessing one's beliefs to confessing one's shortcomings and errors. It shows us once again that we do not know whether there is an original behind this story. The author? Surely Augustine himself. Although, if so, how is he linked to the story? Is there a difference between the story he tells about himself and his 'self'? Or could it be God? If so, can we still talk about an original reality lying behind the text? All these aspects may puzzle the reader, who may be looking for some way out from this labyrinth. Indeed, *Confessions* cannot be considered a kind of diary, only meant to be read by private eyes; no, the picture Augustine drew was intended to become a public one and everyone was invited to read it. At the same time, it was meant to be a picture of himself. However, as Augustine intended

---

[27]'Autobiography' is used for works that received their definite form in the nineteenth century. Think for example, of the great works of Goethe, *Wahrheit und Dichtung*, Proust, *A la recherche du temp perdu*, and Joyce, *A Portrait of the Artist as a Young Man*. Literature about the history of the autobiography is abundant. Cp. J. Brockmeier and D. Carbaugh, *Narrative and Identity: Studies in Autobiography, Self and Culture*, Amsterdam 2001. L. Anderson, *Autobiography*, London 2001. P. J. Eakin, *Living Autobiographically: How We Can Create Identity in Narrative*, Ithaca 2008. R. Folkenflik, ed., *The Culture of Autobiography: Constructions of Self-Representation*, Stanford 1993; Carlo Cristini, Louis Ploton, *Mémoire et autobiographie*, Gerontologie et société 32 (2009) 75–95.

[28]One of the most striking examples of this use of classical elements in an autobiographical work is Gregory of Nazianze, *De Vita Sua*.

[29]See, Carol Harrison, *The Art of Listening in the Early Church*, Oxford 2013, in particular ch. 3 'Images and Echoes', 61–83.

to publish this self-portraiture, this intention radically changed the nature of the picture. Once it has entered the public sphere, it is no longer an epistemological notion in which we are dealing with the difference between image and reality, but it has become a tool in a certain field of public representation. It is like a speech delivered to convince the audience, and that is precisely one of the main features of this old and new genre.[30] It is not meant, in the first instance, to reveal the inner self of the author to his public; it is meant to convince them by telling about oneself. What matters, therefore, is the story, yet this story creates its own reality. Sure, there remains the referential character of the image, but at the same time, the image shows a transformational possibility. It creates its own reality, which is not necessarily identical to the historical truth.[31] This is how, already in Antiquity, writers proved to be familiar with the power of literary images, using their literary technique to bridge the gap between their personal life and their audience. Then, once it has become a reality in the public sphere, it can be adored, criticized, neglected or even despised, which is a fascinating aspect of the autobiographical 'image'. Thus, Augustine created in his *Confessions* an image of himself and, indeed, everyone in the 'audience' (his readers) could value this Augustinian image in their own way.[32] You could love it or adore it, but you could also loathe it and criticize it. Many have venerated it as a unique image of a man who describes his life up to his conversion. They have considered *Confessions* an image that perfectly reflects the inner life of Augustine. Even if this inner

---

[30] Cp. Matthias Smalbrugge, *Autobiography in Classical Times*, forthcoming in the encyclopaedia of Early Christianity.

[31] The best example is the conversion scene in the *Confessions*, already analysed by Pierre Courcelle as mainly a literary fiction. Cp. Pierre Courcelle, *Recherches sur les Confessions de saint Augustin*, Paris 1950, 188–202.

[32] This can be easily discovered when looking at the different biographies of Augustine. There is the famous portrait written by Peter Brown, *Augustine of Hippo: A Biography, new edition*, London 2000 (original version 1967), there is also the much more critical story of James J. O'Donnell, *Augustine. A New Biography*, New York 2005, partially rejecting the vision of Peter Brown, and there is the book of Serge Lancel, much more traditional but also very keen on details, *Saint Augustin*, Paris 1999. See also a new approach, Miles Hollingworth, *Saint Augustine of Hippo: An Intellectual Biography*, London 2013. More recently, Robin Lane Fox added his biography to these important works, called *Augustine: Conversions to Confessions*, New York/London 2015.

life proved to be filled with some elements they strongly rejected, they nonetheless venerated the 'honesty' Augustine practised in *Confessions*. Moreover, qualifying it as 'honest', they suggest they knew the reality Augustine depicted was true. Others stated that it was not an honest image; on the contrary, it was an image made and destined for a certain market. Or, they stated that it could be a 'sentimental journey' to and from one's youth and that it certainly did not necessarily have anything to do with the truth. It was merely a kind of writing that corresponded to Augustine's need to justify his past and make it acceptable in the eyes of his admirers.

Therefore, regardless of whatever preference one may have for this or that 'solution', *Confessions* provides us with an Augustine created by Augustine, and we do not know how the relationship between the author and his work is structured. This is correct, but we do know something else. Augustine raises doubts about the relation between his original self and the story he made out of it. He often raises the question 'why am I doing this, why am I writing about my personal life?', as if the answer could not be found in that personal life itself. Yet, he expressed these doubts intentionally. Indeed, he did not want himself to be the original he was writing about; he wanted God to be the original he was dealing with. In his view, there is no room to talk about a human original, if one has not spoken first of all about God. The divine original precedes every human original, and that was the main goal of *Confessions*, convincing the readers of this absolute priority of God when it comes to speaking of an original. However, we are of course unable to speak about God as God; we must speak about God as he acts in human lives. Hence, *Confessions* spoke about God, but the work did so by telling Augustine's life story. This approach implies a major shift from a normal autobiography, but it entirely preserves the idea of an original behind the story. There is not only the story but also a reality, even a divine one, behind it. It is in this sense that Augustine wrote a unique text that consciously dealt with the question of the relation between image and original. There is no need, at this stage, to dwell further on these questions, but it must be clear that from this moment on, we can no longer talk exclusively about the original – image relationship. We must deal with images that either create new realities or reveal unexpected realities behind the words. We may argue that in general a story is told in a certain way, thus creating certain images that in turn create new stories. The reception of the original story thus becomes the beginning of a new one. *Confessions* is perhaps a striking example of these dynamics. The work has become famous, and many authors have written their own 'confessions', although they did not deal with the question of the original and the image in such an exquisite and subtle way as Augustine. Suffice it to think of the *Monodiae* of Guibert de Nogent, the *De Ascensu Montis Ventosi* of Petrarch and the *Confessions* of Rousseau. In that sense, the autobiography is a fascinating moment in our cultural history, a moment in which there is a kind of dialectical relationship between the story and the reality behind it, as well as the relation between a story and a new story. Indeed, the story can create a new story, and that is what we meet when confronted with parts of the reception of Augustine's autobiography. Nevertheless, this does not imply that the relationship between image and original has changed – it has not. Actually, it is now the story that becomes the original giving birth to a new image, the story about a story.

Concluding remarks about narratives and images

Apparently, however, things have changed. We have lived, up until recent times, in a culture in which the relation between image and the reality behind it was a central theme, with the autobiography being one of the most striking examples of this philosophical and literary play. Even the selfie can be considered a late offspring of these questions. Of course, the selfie was not born nor framed as a new phase in this longstanding history, but the questions that once could be raised were still valid – questions about the relationship between perception and truth, and between perception and narrative. Perception, however, may seem to prevail today, without connecting it any longer to a narrative behind it. That is at least what we see in some forms of politics, which often have been reduced to forms of 'framing'. The story has faded away; we are now dealing with a play without a script. As Nietzsche famously put it, we have wiped out the horizon. This means there is no relation anymore between oneself and a larger narrative. Hence, there is seemingly no reality behind the images we foster so much. Moreover, it seems as if these images are turning themselves against the reality, and as though they want to replace reality by denying it, or by replacing them with 'alternative facts'. The facts do not matter; what matters is the image, which may lead to paramount paradoxes. A museum needs publicity, it needs images in order to show the images of an exhibition. Once you have been convinced by these second-hand images, you enter the museum and you are confronted with images that still try to tell you a story. Looking at an Attic vase with a warrior painted on it, there certainly is a story behind it: a story about love, war, friendship and death. However, we have entered another era in which the link with something to which the image refers seems to be absent. Marketing and branding[33] have become essential features of our society, and though they pretend to tell a story, it is only the product you buy. You do not obtain a story. Therefore, unfortunately, the story has become less important, and you can become president of the United States just by presenting a convincing image. There is no story behind it, not even a trace of a narrative; just a man who consciously reduces his own life to a series of images.[34] Yet, if this is correct, the image is no longer an image, it has become the original it once was considered to reflect.

Three observations must be noted here to be understood correctly. *First* of all, this analysis is not meant to be one of the many complaints about modern society. It certainly does not have the intention to refer to the past as a golden age, the kind of discourse in which analysis and nostalgia team up to become the invincible magic potion of a small village in Gaul. What is intended is to discover how cultural structures are changing, what brought them about and how they can be interpreted. *Secondly*, although the image has become very powerful and 'stories' seem to have become less relevant, this does not imply that there is no need for stories. On the contrary, there still exists this immense desire for stories. There still exists the feeling that image and original, image and reality, image and story should go together. Suffice it to say that the populist movements in Europe all

---

[33]Cp. Lynn R. Kahle, Chung-Hyun Kim, eds., *Creating Images and the Psychology of Marketing Communication*, London 2006.
[34]Maria Elizabeth Grabe, Erik P. Bucy, *Image Bite Politics: News and the Visual Framing of Elections*, Oxford 2010, 57. This is a very illuminating book about the way political stories and convictions have been radically changed into images, leaving very little space to the story, the ideology, of the politician.

tell a story. This may be a story of the past, it may be a story entirely built on nostalgia, but it is a story and it works. Therefore, the desire that once inspired Echo is still present, yet it functions as a symbiotic story in which we can completely identify with the protagonists we admire. *Finally*, though, the most critical question remains the following: If indeed we have moved from a culture that entertains a complex relationship between image and original (implying there has to be a story about the connection between these two elements) to a culture in which the image seems to be the sole reality we have, then what in fact is the overwhelming power of the image? Has it any layers, such as those we can find in the autobiography, and would they be able to explain its attractiveness to us? However, the autobiography is indeed, by its very nature, a play with a script. It deals with the different layers of reality and, even though it presents a certain image of the author, its readers will always be able to grasp a reality behind the words that is different from the image the words intend to shape. The modern image though seems to have another structure, and it is on this relatively new phenomenon that we now must focus. Indeed, a gap exists in our understanding, and it concerns the very dominant character of the image.

If this is correct, and if it might be correct to argue that we may need to go back to the times of Augustine and Ovid to grasp some of the subtleties of the very nature of the image, would it not be worth the trouble to take a closer look at these origins? In particular, should we not try to understand how Augustine thought about the image? No one in Antiquity thought more about the image than Augustine; no one was more able to integrate platonic and Plotinian thoughts on image in rather biblical structures; and no one pictured so sharply the double nature of the image: its reference to the original and its inferiority to it. Therefore, if we want to understand the aforementioned gap, the faultline in our culture, then we should look to this brilliant theologian. Yet, before we can do so, we must analyse the historical background of his ideas on image, and hence, we shall first turn to Plato.

2

The image as a shadow: Plato's cave

The text we shall deal with is the famous *Allegory of the Cave*, figuring in the *Republic*, which was written about 380 BC and is generally considered Plato's most influential work. It deals with the notion of justice and its realization in society and attempts to develop structures in which justice can be realized. To show the structure of realities such as 'justice', Plato speaks in the *Republic* in detail about his theory of Forms. He does so perhaps in the most impressive way in his *Allegory of the Cave*, to be found in book VII: the part in which Glaucon and Socrates continue their discussions. Both men have long been debating the idea of justice, and they have concluded that a philosopher would be the best possible ruler, meaning that he would probably be the most suitable candidate for realizing justice. Notably, in picturing the qualities such a philosopher should have, Plato does not hesitate to clearly allude to his own society, which he describes as profoundly corrupted, where people mainly act out of desire instead of an ideal such as justice or the good. In order, then, to illustrate how such a ruler might act, Socrates, the protagonist, introduces three allegories of which the *Simile of the Cave* is the last. Its main goal is to show how such a philosopher would have to bring about the 'enlightenment or ignorance of our human conditions'. It therefore concerns the educational project that would be most appropriate for teaching, justice, and it runs as follows.¹

At the bottom of a cave, we find people sitting against a wall, tied in such a suffocating way that they cannot even bend their neck and heads. They are sitting next to each other but, as they are so heavily chained, no one can see the others next to him. They are prisoners and unable to escape from this captivity. What is more, they do not long for freedom because they were born in to this situation of captivity. Indeed, one can only long for freedom once one has tasted it. These chained prisoners, therefore, only know their actual, current, state of living and are not aware of their captivity as such. We will come back to this detail later. They can only look right ahead, and what they see in front of them looks to them to be real. It is clear that there is no other reality; there is but one reality – the reality in front of them. They are looking at shadows on the wall in front of them, without knowing that these are only shadows. They are unaware of the fact that behind them is a fire and between the fire and their position people are strolling around, carrying vessels, jugs and all kind of things. Not being able to see these people, they can only see their shadows, projected on the wall of the cave by the light of the fire. This is their sole reality; it is everything they can possibly know. Now imagine, Plato continues, that one of these prisoners was released. That would be a painful experience: one would have to force him, and it would only be unwillingly that he would get up. Yet, once he has stood up, he could be forced to look at the people behind him and to look at the fire. At first, however, he would not be able to look at the fire because his eyes would only be accustomed to the darkness.

---

¹Pol.514a–521b. Cp. Yuji Kurihara, 'Plato on the Ideal of Justice and Human Happiness: Return to the the Cave (Republic 519e–521b)', in Georgios Anagnostopoulos, ed., *Socratic, Platonic and Aristotelian Studies: Essays in Honour of Gerasimos Santos*, London, New York 2011, 271–9; James Wilberding, 'Prisoners and Puppeters in the Cave', *Oxford Studies in Ancient Philosophy* 27(2004), 117–39; T. F. Morris, 'Plato's Cave', *South African Journal of Philosophy* 28(2009), 415–32. Marie-Elise Zovko, 'The Way Up and the Way Back are the Same: Plato's Analogies of the Sun, the Line and the Cave and the Path Intelligence Takes', in *Proceedings of the International Symposium Platonism and Forms of Intelligence*, eds, John Dillon, Marie-Élise Zovko, Akademie Verlag, Berlin 2008, 313–41. Andrew Payne, *The Teleology of Action in Plato's Republic*, Oxford 2017.

Yet once he dared to look at the fire and the people sitting there, he would realize that what he has seen during his whole life had been in fact only shadows, shadows of the objects projected by the light of the fire. The next step would then be that this man would be dragged out from the cave towards the entrance. Just figure, then, that this man would leave his cave behind to walk in the light of the day. He would not immediately be able to do so, however, because the light would blind him. He would stumble and not be able to understand what his eyes were seeing for the first time in his life. Moreover, because he would have to become accustomed to this painful light, he would first of all look at the shadows, which he would still encounter outside the cave. Yet, after a while, he would finally be able to look at the sun and see the light – no longer only as a reflection of itself but as its own reality. He would understand that the sun is the origin of everything we see, meaning that it holds everything that we see together. It brings forth light and, even in the deepest cave, there would be some remnants of this light, allowing poor creatures to see at least something.

The next phase would be that this man would return to the people in the cave in order to tell them about the sun, the light and the shadows. They would not believe him; they would think instead that he had gone mad and that he did not understand reality anymore. Hence, they would finally try to kill him. Although this is rather predictable, and although the man would realize this danger, he, a man who has become acquainted with the truth, has a duty to return to the people in the cave to educate them. This is because the whole story is not about individual wisdom and knowledge of the ultimate Good, but rather about the sake of society at large. This return to the 'blind' people has its parallel in the epistemological turn this unique man has learnt to make. He knows that it was not only his eyes that had to get accustomed to the light; no, it was much more than this single part of his body: it was his whole being. His whole being had to be converted and his eyes were the symbol of this 'conversion' (strepho; 518c). However, this conversion and radical change (metabolè; 516c) are not an individual prerogative; they must be integrated into the whole of society. That is the education philosophers must receive and transmit. There ends the *Simile of the Cave* on education and the different layers of reality. How, then, should we interpret this allegory? Secondary literature focusses mainly on the theory of Forms, on the relation between the Good,² Happiness and Justice, and I will comment regularly on these aspects. Yet there are other aspects that merit specific attention, particularly the elements of the shadow and the Good.

The shadow: A particular image

First of all, there is darkness, in which people can only see shadows and reflections. The terms Plato uses for these reflections are 'skia' (shadow, reflection; 515a; 515d; 516a), 'eidolon' (516a) and 'phantasma' (516b).³ These are words he had already explained in the allegory of the Sun, saying that shadows and reflections belong to the category of 'images' (eikon), which of course cannot be identified with reality itself. The opposition therefore runs between images and reality, between knowledge and opinion and, finally, between freedom and captivity.⁴ What, then, is the shadow? Indeed, the shadow in the platonic view is mainly reduced to something false. It is not the object itself, but rather only an image of it: a shadow. There is, however, a small positive element that still belongs to the shadow, which can have a pedagogical role: once you have learnt to see the shadow as a reflection, you can consider it a stairway to reality. Reality is not isolated, it has its reflections everywhere, and this creates something that could be called a 'lesser' reality. Although the shadow can have a positive function, however, it still represents something false; it is only a reflection of reality. Plato argues that

---

²A detailed discussion is offered by Christopher Rowe, 'The Form of the Good and the Good in Plato's Republic', in Douglas Kern, Fritz-Gregor Hermann, and Terrence Penner, eds., *Pursuing the Good: Ethics and Metaphysics in Plato's Republic*, Edinburgh 2012, 124–53.
³Catherine Collobert, 'The Platonic Art of Myth-Making: Myth as Informative Phantasma', in Catherine Collobert, Pierre Destrée, Francisco J. Gonzalez, eds., *Plato and Myth: Studies on the Use and Status of Platonic Myths*, Leiden/Boston 2012, 87–108, who speaks about the terms *eikon*, *eikasia*, *eidolon* and *phantasma*, stressing that these terms function within the framework of mimesis. She shows how the vocabulary insists on seeing what Plato describes in this myth, reflecting thus the need to 'see' the truth even in a litteral way. Cp. pg. 118–19.
⁴Andrés Fabián Henao Castro, 'Slavery in Plato's Allegory of the Cave: Alain Badiou, Jacques Rancière, and the Militant Intellectual from the Global South', *Theatre Survey* 58(2017) 86–107.

shadows in normal life are often confused with reality and we tend to take them to be something they are not. In other words, they are deceptive and represent erroneous ideas, producing a kind of obscurity and oblivion. Aside from its pedagogical aspect, the shadow, therefore, does not have many positive characteristics, and the best action would be to try to overcome it as soon as possible. Once the shadow has been overcome, it has lost its function and in turn will fall back into the darkness and return to the reign of oblivion. It will no longer exist because we have come to unmask it as an illusion and, once an illusion has been recognized as such, it disappears. It has no longer any function – unless one prefers to stick to this false reality, which might be the case if one is carried away by his desires and loses the capacity to strive towards the truth. Ontologically speaking, however, we should be aware of an interesting aspect: the shadow remains the child of the light. It has no existence outside the realm of light and, although it must be overcome, it nevertheless is – ontologically speaking-part of the light. It is crucial not to ignore this ontological kinship with light, the enigmatic relation between false and true.

Yet, speaking of shadows, the most amazing feature of this shadowy world is the fact that the human beings held captive in this cave should themselves be considered shadows of what a human being can be. These are not the people Plato pictures as an ideal of human life in the *Republic*, the philosophers who know what is true and false. They are only some far-removed shadows of these royal figures, for indeed, Plato clearly describes the ideal of human life, the ultimate reality of human life. That is nothing less than to be a philosopher king. Obvious though this may be, it is something that, to my knowledge, is hardly mentioned in secondary literature. These people have never been close to the ideal of a human being, they are not the ones who, in the prime of their lives, were captured and made into prisoners. No: these people have an inherent inability to attain real knowledge and, as such, they cannot reach full humanness.[5] Although all that is required to achieve the latter

---

[5] There is one exception to this, the intriguing book of Lloyd P. Gerson, *Knowing Persons: A Study in Plato*, Oxford 2006. He explains that the platonic notion of personhood is the idea of the divided person who is always an embodied person. This embodiment impedes our knowledge of the ideal of personhood.

phase of human life is to remember the world of light, they do not do so despite the ability to remember being the only element that still makes them human beings. To a large extent, they have lost their humanity. What is left is only the small chance to go back to this forgotten memory, which might teach them about other forms of reality. There is, therefore, a slight possibility that they will remember that they have to remember. Yet, there is also a puzzling element. If the possibility to remember is all that is left from their humanity, and if memory is so important, what then awakens this memory? How does one remember that one must remember? What could possibly make them aware of another existence? Plato only speaks of the possibility of one of them being 'released' ('lusis'). He even argues that there is a kind of conversion (metastrepho; 518d) of the whole mind – but by whom or by what is this conversion realized? Indeed, if someone were to be released, what would make him discover his memory, as well as the fact that there is more than just a series of images? For, even if one no longer sees the the shadows, there is no reason to doubt their existence and reality. As one has been a shadow oneself, can one conclude this characteristic has entirely vanished once one has started to remember? Thus, the most striking effect in this allegory is perhaps the fact that, sure, the text confronts us with an ontology showing the difference between the world of light and that of darkness; however, it does not speak of the apparent lack of reality and of truth that pervades these human beings, who have either lost their humanness, or who never had it in the first place. *The real shadows are not the shadows of the vessels and objects that are worn around; the real shadows are these people.* This raises the following question: the shadows of which Plato speaks are the shadows of real objects, such as vessels, but if these human beings are the real shadows, then what kind of being do they reflect as a shadow? Of what are they the shadows? Are they shadows without being the shadow of something? One might suggest that they reflect the perfect philosopher, the one who knows reality. But then we are talking of a being who has been able to free himself of all misunderstanding, of opinions that for so long had prevailed against knowledge. We are talking of someone who has been educated, and who has been capable of raising himself to a certain standard of knowledge. Someone who used his capacities – yet where do these capacities come from; where does memory start? – to raise himself to the standards of justice, of the Good and so on. Yet he cannot be a mixture of knowledge of good, justice, beauty and so on. As a man, he must have his own essence, his own ideal. To put this differently: what was the inner truth, the ideal man, that made the philosopher become a philosopher? Did his memory show him the ideal man just as it shows us the ideal table? From where did that memory come? Is there any Form of man? For indeed, if justice refers to the ultimate justice, and if the good is only good by reflecting the ultimate good, what then is the ultimate man? That is the question with which the shadow, the image, confronts us.

The moral problem: What is the image an image of?

The second element that strikes us in the allegory of the Cave is the (re-)turn to the Good. The ultimate Good is what man must look for and which, fortunately, is also accessible. At least it seems to be for the man who leaves the Cave behind and sees the Sun. Sure, enormous efforts are required to see where the real Good is situated, and to break away from the shadows that so easily seduce our consciousness and trouble our knowledge. Yet, at least according to this story, man is capable of climbing out of the obscurity in which he lay down, bound and unable to see anything other than reflections. Once this prisoner has been loosened – and, once again, Plato does not tell us how it happens but describes it as a rather passive process of people being forced – he can climb out of the cave and see reality as it is. Finally, he will even be able to see the Sun, to enjoy its light and discover the ultimate Good.[6] The discovery of the Good shows us that there is a kind of inner longing for the Good, and this longing coincides with our personal

---

[6] Which is not the same as a happy life. Socrates explains elsewhere that the good in our daily lives, is a mixture of reason, beauty, harmony, proportionality and truthfulness. See, John M. Cooper, 'Plato and Aristotle on "Finality" and (Self-) Sufficiency', in John M. Cooper ed., *Knowledge, Nature and the Good: Essays on Ancient Philosophy*, Princeton 2004, 270–308, in particular 277–9.

capacities. We can live a good life and this capacity never gets lost;[7] the Good is something that is accessible, in a way. That is what this story seems to tells us. It seems to be a story about our capacities, about the ultimate Good we can attain. Yet the questions remain of what exactly is this element that awakens man. How does he begin to see the difference between the good and lesser goods? What kissed his memory awake? Thus, how did we come to remember that we must remember? Plato does not answer the question – although it remains a crucial one. What he argues is that every part of reality is linked to the Good. In the last and first instance, every reality is, to some extent, penetrated by the Good and will therefore always remain related to the Good. But is it then correct to argue that the purest being, the Good, is obscured and that the only requirement is to simply rediscover the way out of the cave, towards the light – towards the Sun? For, once again, what has made us remember that we have to remember? Is it acceptable to think that decay and evil represent only corrupted parts of being that, even in their worst forms, still contain germs of the Good? The notion of the shadow seems to suggest such a solution, as the shadow is always part of the light. Indeed, normally speaking, shadows do not behave independently. Hence the Good remains visible, even in the worst obscurity. Even if the shadow looks dark and seems to lack the light, it remains the child of the light. We are still speaking of one sole reality. This reality may be fractured, it may contain superior or inferior layers, but it has nevertheless preserved its unity. This is an optimistic model in which even the worst darkness still remains related to the light. Secondly, although Plato pictures mankind, even in its worst form, as related to the Good, and although moral questions do have an ontological nature, we should not forget that the shadows are turning to the Good. This means that the question of the shadow as an image of the Good also qualifies the whole problem of the image as a moral one. The shadows are asking for justice, for a morality that chases away the darkness of the Cave.

---

[7]Plato insists on the fact that indeed we are talking about an innate capacity: *enousan dunamin* (518c). This innate capacity even never loses its power: *dunamin oudepote apollusin* (518e). See, Daniel Russel, 'Pleasure and Moral Psychology in Republic IV and IX', in, Daniel Russel ed., *Plato on Pleasure and the Good Life*, Oxford 2005, 106–36.

This, however, is exactly where the problem starts. The Cave is a description of slavery, of utter dependence and constraint, which Plato explains by arguing that we are enslaved by our desires, by our mean passions and our constant longing for material well-being. Yet does this explanation suffice? Is it plausible to suppose that these mean desires have locked us up into a kind of Cave from where any escape is impossible? Either these prisoners were born prisoners or they have started their lives in relative freedom but, somewhere and somehow, they have ended up as prisoners. If they were born prisoners, the idea of someone escaping from this horrible condition would be rather implausible, because their nature would not offer them the possibility of thinking of something other than their actual existence in the Cave. Life, in that case, would not have started with Light but rather darkness, and the idea of an existence being essentially related to the light (as a shadow must be) would be incorrect. But then again, if the beginning of life must be situated within the realm of Light, of which we remain necessarily the shadows, would it never have occurred to anyone that he has become enslaved by his passions? Furthermore, would he not be longing – even though perhaps he is not capable of attaining it – for the Light? The conclusion must be that the platonic picture of this life lived in a Cave does not explain away the terrible force that has made us prisoners in such a way that even the longing for light, for some tiny trace of remembrance, has definitely vanished. There is an unnamed force which is perhaps more essential to our shadowy existence than Plato would admit. This is what Plato is hiding in his story. He does not explain the rise and decline of humankind. All he offers are the foul desires that explain the downturn of human beings, and memory as access to an unexpected conversion, but there is no further analysis: neither of the power of these fatal desires nor of the origin of the salvational memory. Neither does he explain why the prisoner is not only driven to the darker sides of life but has also become enslaved to the point of being incapable of moving. This means any conversion is impossible. Obviously, there is a hidden force that either acts in a positive way (when it makes us remember that we have to remember) or in a negative way (when it leaves us in a state of absolute oblivion), reducing us utterly to passive prisoners, incapable of freeing ourselves. What he mentions is only that someone can be forced ('anagkazo!'; 515c) to raise, to turn himself to the light and to see.

This hidden part of the shadow is not only visible by its absence in Plato's epistemology, it also seems to have been confirmed by our own experiences of the last two centuries. Although rationalism took a solid foothold after the French Revolution, we have become increasingly aware of the fact that the shadow is not merely the lesser part of a golden reality. On the contrary, it is another reality, breaking into pieces our idea of one united, albeit fractured, reality.[8] What we have seen in the last centuries are shadows moving independently from any good. These are shadows who in no sense are orphans of the light; they are not connected to the light at all. It is the pure absence of justice, times that speak of the 'banality of evil'[9] instead of 'the fragility of goodness'.[10] What we discovered was a reality of Evil that had no connection to morals, to the truth, to justice. For a long time, we have lived with the idea of one sole reality that, even if it was fractured and layered, remained a unity in which the lowest parts were still related to the Good, thus forming one sole reality. That model seems to have collapsed and we suddenly have been confronted with an unexpected alternate reality. We have now met in our history shadows that can hardly be called children of the light. Regardless, then, of any objective or subjective character of the Good, these shadows exist and indeed move outside the realm of the Good. They are no longer shadows in the traditional sense of the word, for they act without relation to the Good. They are shadows, but they are no longer shadows of the Light. What then are they the shadows of? Their being can no longer be situated within the platonic ontology, so what is their ontic characteristic? What we are confronted with, therefore, are shadows that were – and still are – very difficult to understand, and their dynamics seem to be inaccessible to any platonic epistemology.

---

[8]The simile of the Cave evokes an allegory of the Hades, as has been pointed out many times. Cp. 'Spectacles from Hades: On Plato's Myths and Allegories in the Republic', in, Catherine Collobert, ed., *Plato and Myth*, Leiden/Boston 2012, 109–24.

[9]Cp. Hanna Arendt, *Eichmann in Jersusalem: A Report on the Banality of Evil*, London 1963.

[10]Cp. Martha Nussbaum, *The Fragilty of Goodness: Luck and Ethics in Greek Tragedy and Philosophy*, Cambridge 2001.

There is still another difficulty. Although we have discovered the fundamentally non-rational character of our reality, and although we became aware of the fact that reason and the good were not always identical, this lack of identity turned out to be even more frightening than we could imagine. The shadows we have experienced in recent times were not completely the opposite of rationality; on the contrary: warfare, torture, genocide all happened in an extremely rational way and had extremely rational reasons – and that is not a pleonasm – capable of justifying the acts.[11] This, perhaps, is one of the main reasons it is so difficult to recognize the shadow as a shadow. We are accustomed to identifying rationality with the good — thanks to Plato; thanks to the Enlightenment – but even the irrational, even the shadow, can be dressed up in rational garb. What is hiding behind this rational and rationalistic outlook, however, is difficult to understand. We fail to understand what is happening, we fail to understand and master ourselves because,[12] even in the worst cases of evil behaviour, there still should be, in our traditional platonic way of thinking, a relationship with the good. As this is not the case, what then has happened, and what do we not know of that which we ought to know? We do not have

---

[11] Apart from the example Hannah Arendt gave in her *Eichmann in Jerusalem: A Report on the Banality of Evil*, New York 1963, there is the striking example of how the the elimination of the Jews was hided and disguised as an idealistic project with an almost eschatological perspective: building a new city instead of old ones, characterized by ghettos. The project implied founding Litzmannstadt, a new livelily city full of happy young people, designed by outstanding architects instead of Lodz (the name Lodz was replaced by the Nazis in 1939). The project that was even filmed, though the movie was never finished. Cp. J. Gordon Horowitz, *Gettostadt: Lodz and the Making of a Nazi City*, Harvard 2009, 123–4.

[12] This could be called a case of 'akrasia', but I wouldn't put in these terms. *Akrasia* refers to a state of mind in which we lose our mind. A kind of lack of self-knowledge, which situates *akrasia* in fact from the very beginning in the realm of rationality. Cp. Chris Bobonich, 'Plato on Akrasia and Knowing Your Own Mind', in, Christopher Bobonich and Pierre Destrée, eds., *Akrasia in Greek Philosophy: From Socrates to Plotinus*, Leiden/Boston 2007, 40–60, which maintains this rational outlook. For the opposite view, that akrasia was not acceptable to Plato, see Donald Davidson, 'Plato's Philosopher', in, Terence Irwin and Martha C. Nussbaum, eds., *Virtue, Love & Form: Essays in Memory of Gregory Vlastos*, Edmonton, Alberda 1993, 179–94; 181. I would conclude that the possibility of *akrasia* seems at last to be accepted by Plato.

an epistemology capable of understanding the reality behind the Good and Rational.[13] Be it inside or outside us, this knowledge situates itself outside the realm of our ordinary knowledge, and we do not know how to get acquainted with it. We have no access to this unknowable realm; we are hardly even aware of its existence. That is what we see in the allegory of the Cave. We are looking at people who are captured, who are prisoners in a hidden prison, incapable of loosening their chains. What has happened to their capacities, to their reason? It is a fate that seems inaccessible to our reason.[14] There is ignorance because we have not yet developed an epistemology capable of understanding a reality that has nothing to do with the Good. It is a reality giving rise to vice and badness,[15] a reality that completely contradicts our normal optimism. This optimism is based on the idea that there will always exist a link with the realm of the Good. That is not the case. All now boils down to the conclusion that there is a reality which we still call 'shadow', but which has no relation whatsoever with the light, and which is not the reflection of a higher reality. The conclusion must now be that, although very well disguised and veiled, we are confronted with

---

[13] Of course, we are not dealing here with a kind of Manicheistic thinking. Manicheism is strongly aware of the presence of Evil and pretends to have knowledge of this Evil. The problem in Manicheism is not the knowledge of something that is hidden, but the battle between Good and Evil. Moreover, Manicheism considers Good and Evil to be external realities, acting on human beings, but not representing inner forces. Plato's philosophy of image confronts us with a domain we can hardly investigate.

[14] Vasili Politis focusses on this *aporia* of man, knowing that he knows not and tries to understand this *aporia* in highlighting the role of the allegory of the Sun. Vasili Politis, 'The *Aporia* in the *Charmides* about Reflexive Knowledge and the Contribution to Its Solution in the Sun Analogy of the *Republic*', in Douglas Cairns, Fritz-Gregor Hermann, and Terrence Penner, eds., *Pursuing the Good: Ethics and Metaphysics in Plato's Republic*, Edinburgh 2012, 231–50.

[15] Verity Harte, in a beautiful article, describes this ignorance which is not the absence of knowledge, but the contrary of knowledge. In her own words: 'First, ignorance, as I have argued, is not simply the absence of something – of knowledge or true belief: it is a state of being possessed of some false impression about the world that is actively endorsed. Second, ignorance does not simply consist in the soul's active endorsement of some single false impression regarding some narrowly specific aspect of the world: ignorance is a standing complex condition of the soul as a whole. To be more specific about what this complex condition is, is not straightforward'. See, Verity Harte, Melissa Lane, eds., *Politeia in Greek and Roman Philosophy*, Princeton 2013, 139–54, p. 149.

images of which we do not know the original they reflect. They are shadows, but the shadows of what, in fact?

The return of the philosopher

The last element we should examine is the fact that the philosopher, once he has discovered the truth, must unexpectedly return to his companions in the cave. Socrates's partner, Glaucon, protests and says that you can hardly consider this descent as something 'just'. Is it not true that we are finally talking about a man who recently discovered the truth? How then can we possibly oblige him to return to the realm of the shadows and leave the truth behind? That would not only be absurd but also something unjust – unjust to the philosopher, for it is not just to oblige someone to return to a world of falsehood. Such a man would fail to do justice to himself and, for that reason, there is no possibility of returning to the cave once one has discovered the truth. This argument sounds plausible, yet Socrates rejects it. Justice does not only concern the individual; it is also a societal question. A man who has discovered the truth, not because he was so talented that he became 'self-evidently' aware of it but because he has been forced to climb out of the cave, should also behave on behalf of the whole of society[16]:

> 'You have forgotten again, my dear friend,' I said, that this is not the purpose of the law that a single section of the community will do exceptionally well, but the intention is that this will apply across the whole state by uniting the populace by persuasion and compulsion, and by making them share the services with each other which every individual can do for the common good; and the law itself can create such people in our state, not to allow

---

[16]Michael Cloete, 'Revisiting Plato's Republic: Towards a Praxis of Justice', *Phronimon* 11 (2010) 65–79. The author rejects the 'totalitarian' interpretation of Karl Popper and states that, in our modern times with so many people living in circumstances to be compared with those in the cave, we should even more value the idea of justice Socrates formulated in the *Republic*.

each person to turn whichever way he wants, but so it can make full use of them in binding the whole state together.[17]

The reason a philosopher has to return to the cave is the common good, which represents justice – although we should not forget that the philosopher who returns to the cave is not obliged to stay there for the rest of his life. He will stay there for a certain amount of time before someone else can take over his task. For the philosopher himself has also an obligation to nourish his own soul with truth and to live in the light. He has a twofold life: one on behalf of society, and one on behalf of his personal interests.[18] The philosopher's return to the cave and to his former fellow-prisoners is necessary in order to build a society worthy of its name. Otherwise, society will be taken over by men who only look after their own interests, which Plato describes as follows:

> *If you get, in public affairs, men who are so morally impoverished that they have nothing they can contribute themselves, but who hope to snatch some compensation for their own inadequacy from a political career, there can be no good government. They start fighting for power, and the consequent internal and domestic conflicts ruin both them and society.*[19]

This biting commentary could easily be applied to our modern society. Apparently, there is also another way of living a shadowy life, according to Plato. There is not only the poor prisoner, who is unable to move and will probably always live in the darkest circumstances possible, but there is also the other side: those who can only think of their personal interests and who are entirely morally corrupted, in Plato's view. They live like predators, taking what does not belong to them, practising injustice as if it were justice. Because they were elected, they were indeed chosen to govern. But, as they cannot govern themselves, they cannot govern society in the right way. In fact, they are also prisoners; not only are we confronted with the mob

---

[17] Translation Loeb edition, Cambridge 2013.
[18] Yuji Kurihara, 'Plato in the Ideal of Justice and Human Happiness: Return to the Cave (Republic 519e–521b)', in, G. Anagnostopoulos ed., *Socratic, Platonic and Aristotelian Studies: Essays in Honor of Gerasimos Santas*, University of California, San Diego, 271–9.
[19] Translation H. D. P. Lee.

– whom you might easily consider slaves of their desires, living in complete darkness – but also the governing body, which lives no less in frightening blindness. Plato's description leaves us with the idea that human existence does not easily lead to the truth. For, whereas in books II and III of the *Republic* he could suggest that the various shortcomings of the arts could easily be corrected, it now turns out to be much more difficult. Why? Because it is our nature itself that misleads us. It is in our nature that we meet ourselves, playing in forbidden stories we have written ourselves. It is not the story that is disturbing: it is the author. This seems to be the discovery of book VII.

That is also the problem with the philosopher returning to the cave. He cannot explain what has happened, neither to himself nor to the others, but simultaneously he fiercely rejects the life and knowledge of the prisoners. He points at the images, explaining that he and his fellow-prisoners have become images and shadows themselves, yet he is incapable of explaining what kind of ideal they, as human beings, are considered the reflection of. Nor is he able to explain why all these people find themselves back in this prison called the Cave. Therefore, in the end he is not able to explain who he is himself and what the essence of his existence might be. Even the philosopher does not know the truth.[20] This comes down to concluding, as we already mentioned, that images do not only reveal something, but also hide something. Although

---

[20] A well-known interpretation if of course the one given by Heidegger, stating that the real sense of truth(a-letheia) is the disclosure of reality, as he gave it in his lectures from 1933, *Sein und Wahrheit*, recently translated as *Being and Truth*, Bloomington 2010. See, e.g., James N. McGuirk, 'Aletheia and Heidegger's Transitional Readings of Plato's Cave Allegory', *Journal of the British Society for Phenomenology* 39(2008) 167–85, who emphasizes that finally Heidegger wasn't able to live with an acceptable interpretation of the Cave allegory – not withstanding his interpretation of aletheia – and therefore 'fled into poetry'. Heideggers interpretation does not match the rest of Plato's argument. It does not counter the difficulties with the notion of the One (the Truth) and its relations with the Many. It seeks its essence in the revelation of the truth but does not care about the unity of the hidden, the concealed and the revealed. Jan Szaif on the other hand approaches truth as a notion with a double meaning. On the one hand it is an ideal at an ontological level, on the other hand it is the capability of discerning what is correct. Truth therefore is opposed to 'ametria' (486d). This seem a much more fruitfull approach than the one Heidegger proposed. See, Jan Szaif, 'Die Alêtheia in Platons Tugendlehre', in, Marcel Van Ackeren, ed., *Platon verstehen. Themen und Perspektiven*, Darmstadt 2004, 183–209.

our ignorance can partially be removed by climbing the stairs to the light, there remains ignorance about the shadowy side of our reality. Therefore, although Plato suggests that what remains invisible in the image is a higher reality, this seems to be an overly optimistic view. What is hidden, what remains invisible, is also a reality full of violence, of hate and destruction, which is not due to the image itself and its defective nature. It would be unjust to state that the defectiveness of the image is the cause of this negative reality. On the contrary, it is the opposite: its defective nature is the result of a 'lower' reality it has to cover up. Apparently, the possibility also exists that the image reflects another reality to an ideal one. These are questions Plato leaves unanswered and that keep us puzzled. We have discovered that the image can be seen as a shadow – often the shadow of the good, but often also the shadow of a reality we do not know. Hence, the ontological question of the image therefore also has a strong moral nature. If we ultimately do not know what our deepest essence is, what we are striving for and why we do so, one could easily conclude that we lack a sense of inner unity. Ontologically speaking, we are not able to see what the ultimate role of the ideal is, and from where the ideal takes its ideal form. Moreover, we have discovered images and shadows of Evil, which could not be related to the Good, entailing a division of our reality into two separate parts. Once again, I am not trying to introduce any kind of Manichaeism, but rather only to consider a vacuum Plato seems to have created.

3

Augustine and the broader focus on image

The thorny question of the image and its double nature,[1] the void Plato had discovered but could not solve – this is what Augustine struggled with his whole life. Indeed, the double nature of the image was what he mostly tried to understand. How was it possible that man, on the one hand, was created in the image of God, while on the other hand could seemingly live as if there were no God? What, then, is the nature of the image? Can one be born with a certain image and lose it? Or is it impossible to lose the divine image according to which we have been created? If so, what does this imply? Does it mean that we remain 'enlightened' by this divine image, or is this image comparable to the platonic memory, something that can be entirely forgotten and that no longer has an effective presence in our lives.

These are the questions Augustine struggled with and, as is well known, they were far from merely theoretical for him, which is why he was able to take such a step forward in defining the problem of the image. What Augustine did was to apply the whole question of the image to the question of the nature of language and theology. Allow me to explain: thinking about the Word and God, about the Word that became flesh, Augustine had to think about the relationship between language and the divine reality,

---

[1] Cp. Matthew Drever, *Image, Identity and the Forming of the Augustinian Soul*, Oxford 2013.

which he did in a fascinating way. Of course, one might argue that Plato had already studied this relationship, particularly in the *Parmenides*, where he dared to call into question his own theory of Forms and Ideas. Augustine was probably influenced by the ideas Plato developed in the *Parmenides*, but his own angle was a different one. Unlike Plato, he did not focus on the notion of unity and plurality, but rather on incarnation. This incarnation was not a representation of a lower reality, but one of the ultimate reality in which image and divine reality become one. Fascinated as he was by questions surrounding the image, Augustine did not consider them merely theoretical. On the contrary, he recognized all the aspects of the notion of image – the possible loss of, as well as identification with, the divine – in his personal life; therefore, his theology of image is also an endeavour to define the very nature of theology itself. Is this only the theoretical reasoning about God and human life, or is it also a reflection of our personal lives? Put another way: is theology itself an image of a certain reality, and does it therefore possess a certain ontological, even incarnational, character? This is the fascinating question we must deal with when we delve into Augustine's thoughts on the image. It is one of the greatest aspects of his theology that he dared to connect the notion of the image to his personal life and created from this his theology. He made it clear that, once one studies the question of the theology of image by focusing on one's personal life, one's theology is not necessarily personalized, but rather addresses the question of the incarnational nature of theology itself. The *Confessions*, therefore, is not simply the autobiography we usually consider it, and neither is it simply a *paraenesis* destined to show that a man cannot discover his own inner life without turning himself to God: it is no less an endeavour to see whether a personal focus on the theology of image can teach us something about the incarnational nature of theology itself.

This turn in Augustine's thought is so critical that it exceeds all the questions about 'what is true in the *Confessions*, and what is fiction' and so on. The real point is that Augustine, thinking on the nature of theology, saw no way other than speaking and writing about himself. That is what makes his theology of image such a vital topic: it deals with the very nature of our thinking – and not even our thinking in general, but rather our thinking about God. What Augustine wondered is whether theology is only a theoretical framework that is more or less plausible, or whether it might also be an image of the relationship between God and man. This means that the theology of image is a particularly exciting subject. Indeed, could it possibly be true that theology is not only a reflection on human existence and its relationship with God, but that as a reflection it is itself part of this relationship? It would, as it were, be the unfolding of this relationship. If that were true, the theology of image would almost be a pleonasm. Moreover, theology would be an analogy of the prologue of St John, where the 'Word became flesh'. Every theology, in that case, is an image of the relationship between God and man. It is part of the incarnation, implying that the notion of participation is also an important one. What participation really is needs to be explained later, but if it is a valid one in Augustine's view, then thinking about God is already sharing part of his being. In that case, theology is not a merely a theoretical framework; it is part of the incarnation, and it participates in the reality it reflects.

However, this reflection is of course only an incomplete one. There is some similitude, but also dissimilarity; it is an image but, as such, it can only partly reflect the original. All these notions must therefore be studied. We must discover what similitude is, what participation is, and whether it matches with the idea that, somewhere, the dissimilarity must have a cause that is not directly visible, but which will nevertheless make us aware of something we might also call 'reality' – albeit a dark, hidden one. It is therefore critical that Augustine studied these notions of similarity and dissimilarity in many of his works, in order to understand how we can or cannot resemble a certain reality. Turning to these notions broadens the scope Plato presented, and it is Augustine's main contribution to the notion of image. Therefore, we will concentrate on these notions in order to understand how Augustine viewed 'image'.

The platonic background

Given the previous chapters, the first question will now be whether we can find some traces of Plato in Augustine's writings. The answer has for long stated the obvious: yes there are many traces of Plato's philosophy. They are mostly considered to be Neoplatonist traces, stemming from Plotinus[2] and Porphyry, but even though scholars mostly agree on the Neoplatonist aspect of these traces, the question remains how far this influence pervades the theology of Augustine. Some would suggest that it is a lasting influence that always resurfaces in Augustine's thinking, whereas others would argue that Augustine's thinking had become so profoundly Christian that it produced a rift between the early works, still largely influenced by Neoplatonist thinking, and the later works, evidently Christian. We will not enter this debate, although the question of identity was indeed an important one in the days of Augustine – suffice it to think of the great debate between Ambrose and Symmachus on the altar of Victoria. Nevertheless, the notion of identity is perhaps not the most fruitful approach when speaking about the image. Both notions seem to exclude one another. An image is something fluid; it can change, its form never definite, whereas identity seems to be – at least until recent times[3] – a notion characterized by a certain stability, or even by a fixed shape. By not taking into account the fact that the identity and image are partly identical, and that they are both fluid notions, we risk falling into the trap of an anachronistic debate on identity.

This being said, the Neoplatonist influence in Augustine's works is an important one, and it is worth making some brief observations on this influence with respect to the notion of image. It is through studying Plato that Augustine became aware of the importance of the notions of participation, similarity and dissimilarity. We can discover some aspects of these first steps in this epistemological field in *Confessions*. He mentions, in book VII

---

[2] Cp. Michel Fattal, *Plotin chez Augustin. Suivi de Plotin face aux Gnostiques*, Paris 2006.

[3] The modern debate on identity and its newly discovered fluid character, seemingly has not yet influenced patristic studies. Since Alfaric, the question was all about the Neoplatonist character of Augustine's theology. In fact the discussion never stopped and can still be found back in the works of Lewis Ayres and Carol Harrison. One of the best introductions in this very complicated matter is Ronnie J. Rombs, *Saint Augustine and the Fall of the Soul: Beyond O'Connel and His Critics*, Catholic University of America Press 2006.

of *Confessions*, the Platonists books he has read, introducing this passage by another discovery. For already, in book VI, he describes how, while listening to the sermons of St Ambrose, he understood that Scripture speaks of men being created in the image of God. It suddenly strikes him, thanks to the preaching of Ambrose, that one cannot possibly conceive this image to be a physical one. Such an immaterial view was opposed to what he had learned from the Manichaeans, namely that God could be imagined as a kind, elevated human being. Once he has understood the immaterial nature of this divine image, he wonders why, somewhat earlier, he arrogantly pretended to understand what was meant by 'in the image of God', for he did not know at all what it meant.[4] He then leaves the question about the nature of this image unanswered, in order to take it up again in the next book. There, however, the setting has changed. It is no longer St Ambrose who awakens his insight; it is the collection of books of the so-called Platonists that offer him valuable and very precious insights. These books – which still cannot be completely identified, but are most probably Neoplatonist books, in particular those of Plotinus[5] and Porphyry – will teach him that in the beginning, the Word was with God and the Word was God. They also teach him that God's progeny is not the fruit of carnal desire, but that it was born of God himself. Yet Augustine writes that essential differences remain between the Christian message and these platonic books: the most important being that the name of Christ is entirely lacking in the books. This is not just a pious remark, a *captatio benevolentiae*, it concerns the possibility or impossibility of being completely similar to God or not. That is how Augustine will develop his Christology: by speaking about a complete similarity between the Father and the Son.

However, what also mattered was that Plato taught him that the divine image, according to which man was created, can simply be deformed. Moreover, the divine image can easily be identified with a perishable man, or even 'bent' into the image of an animal.

---

[4] *Conf.* VI,4,5.
[5] Cp. *De Beata Vita* I,4: *Lectis autem Plotini paucissimis libris.*

In other words, the divine image torn down, it can be spoiled and even be lost.[6] He is even more explicit when he combines this philosophical approach with biblical language, quoting *Romans* 1,25 by saying that humans are capable of distorting the divine image into one of a ruminating cow. That is, of course, a spectre he would never wish to come true. Had he, on the contrary, succumbed to such a view, this would have been nothing else than what he calls, 'tasting the Egyptian dishes'. The metaphor is a clear one and it wraps up the philosophical heritage taken from these books of the Platonists in a biblical narrative. These 'dishes' allude to the story of the Jewish people who, wandering in the desert and almost starving to death, longed for the comfort and the food of the Egyptian life they had left behind. Well, adds Augustine, I, fortunately, did not succumb to that kind of temptation. The underlying suggestion is clear and matches the following verses in the first chapter of Paul's Epistle to the *Romans*: the Jewish people turned down their heritage, they have lost their soul. Yet this soul, now spoiled, is nothing other than the precious bond between man and God. What is the essence of this bond? It is the living memory of the fact that man is created in the image of God. This image, however, is an immaterial one and a Christian should never take it in a more material sense. If that were the case, one would abuse this notion and misunderstand what similarity and dissimilarity are when it comes to the relationship between God and man.

That is Augustine's technique in the *Confessions*: wrapping up philosophical issues in biblical narratives. The whole picture in fact comes down to the platonic scheme we have analysed above, this time combined with some strong elements of anti-Judaism: human beings are gifted with the memory of the truth, of the Good, of the divine, which makes them images of God; yet this does not guarantee that they will take care of this precious heritage. On the contrary, they can also end up as prisoners of lower desires. What Augustine emphasizes, therefore, is the fact that already in the platonic heritage one can find the idea of mankind losing its soul due to a longing for lower desires. There is an imbalance between similarity and dissimilarity and, fortunately, the same pattern can

---

[6]*Conf.* VII,9,15.

be found in the Bible. So, indeed, the negative side has become visible and it finds its inspiration partly in the platonic tradition, while also wrapped up in some biblical images. This downfall of the soul was only part of the story, however. It was the first step made by Augustine in identifying the reason why the divine image can be lost, or at least why it can temporarily disappear. Indeed, it is clear that the platonic tradition taught Augustine that such a loss was far from improbable. But there is also the other side of the coin, upon which he expands in *De Ciuitate Dei*. There Augustine insists on the possibility of being similar to God and argues that this is already to be found in Plato. His 'review' of Plato is a positive one overall, and he argues that Plato at least recognized that the Good and the divine cannot be something material. No, there is a light that has to be the origin of all living creatures and that illuminates all reasonable thinking.[7] It is for this reason that Plato deserves to be praised above all the other philosophers. To put it even more clearly: Platonists conceive of God in the following terms: He is *causa subsistendi, ratio intellegendi* and *ordo vivendi*[8]: the cause of existence, the ground of understanding and the order of life. There is even more: Plato argues that the philosopher loves God because he recognizes that God is the ultimate Good. So, if he loves God, he also enjoys Him.[9] Therefore, one might even think that Plato has read the Bible. He is so close, in his philosophy, to phrases such as 'I am who I am' (Ex. 3),[10] that one could easily think of some biblical inspiration for the Platonist's view. Yet however serious that praise may be, it can only be limited one and once again we meet the text of *Romans* 1. Even the Platonists continued to stick to the wrong images, and unfortunately they belonged to those who turn the image of the immortal and immaterial God into images of the gods as mortal men.[11] That is why the Greeks, even the Platonists, fail to share in the ultimate truth. That is what Augustine reproaches Plato with in the end. Plato had discovered, says Augustine, that the ultimate Good could not be conceived of

---

[7] *De Ciu.* VIII,4.
[8] *De Ciu.* VIII,4.
[9] *De Ciu.* VIIII,8.
[10] *De Ciu.* VIII,11.
[11] *De Ciu.* VIII,10.

as something material. Why, then, did he still continue to believe that there were many gods, and that these gods, although of course representing the Good, had material forms? Besides, is it not ridiculous to believe in those gods once one has discovered that there is only one divine Good? It is in these lines that we come across Augustine's enormous appreciation of Plato, as well as his aversion to Plato's philosophy. His platonic background taught him about the possibilities of similarity and dissimilarity. Similarity must be based on participation with the divine, and this positive approach will always linger in his thoughts. The same appreciation is brought to the fore in *De Vera Religione* III,3, where Augustine suggests that his readers imagine what Plato's answers would have been had he still lived: *si enim Plato ipse viveret*. Both aspects are largely dealt with in *De Ciuitate Dei*, but these discussions do not concern the specific problem of the image. It is for this reason that we will not examine these books in detail. May it suffice to point out that Augustine frequently refers to the platonic inspiration of his theology but that, when alluding to Plato or the Platonists, he mainly mentions the headlines of the platonic system without referring in detail to the notion of image. What he learned was the imbalance between being similar to the divine, and being estranged from it. In the end, while Plato was extremely important, Augustine would develop his own notion of image, focusing increasingly on the notions of similarity and dissimilarity. How did he proceed?

First of all, although the platonic influence is quite clear, it may seem as if this influence mainly concerns the image being taken as the image of God. In a way this is correct, but the image, while also having ordinary meanings, is much more. Augustine uses it to speak about dreams, impressions, memories of what he has seen or what he remembers images stemming from images and so on. There is a whole world of images and they greatly differ one from another. The images we see in our dreams are entirely different from those kept in our memory. There are visual images such as pictures, mental images such as dreams, and all these images are like different universes in which one can walk around. One looks at them, sometimes frightened, sometimes delighted, but the question will always be how real all these images are. That goes for the picture as well as for the dream; one wants to know whether these images have any resemblance to reality. This question is not one that simply passes by as a kind of casual thought. No, it is the first and most important question we deal with when it comes to images: how real are they – to what extent do they resemble the reality they reflect? In other words, we must know more about similitude because that that is the notion on which images are based: there must be a kind of similitude between the image and that which it reflects.[12] However, speaking about similitude also implies speaking about dissimilarity and it is on these notions I would like to focus.[13]

The main aspects of image: Similarity and dissimilarity

Similitude – what is it about? Augustine studied this question intensively, and he dealt with it in different books. It starts in the *Soliloquies*, where he attempts to discover the main characteristics of similitude. The *Soliloquies* are a kind of inner dialogue[14] between Augustine and his Reason, which is why it is called *Soliloquia* (a conversation with oneself). In this book, Reason is the critical partner of Augustine, who constantly questions him about his thoughts, feelings and convictions. It is a highly critical conversation in which Augustine often has to admit that his original point of view was not correct. Although the book – Augustine's second publication[15] – mainly deals with the question of knowledge of God and the soul, it also addresses the question of similitude. It does so by introducing in the first chapter the difference between similar,

---

[12] A very instructive article remains the one of R. A. Markus, '"Imago" and "similitudo" in Augustine', *REAug* 10(1964) 125–43 in which he explains the influence of Marius Victorinus and the distinction Augustine maintained between *imago* and *similitudo*, as well as the passage from *ad imaginem dei* to *imago Dei*.
[13] Cp. Jérôme Lagouanère, *Intériorité et réflexivité dans la pensée de Saint Augustin: Formes et genèse d'une conceptualisation*, Paris 2012. See, the rather negative review by J. M. Rist, *Journal of Theological Studies* 65(2014)309–12. Isabelle Bochet, 'Le statut de l'image dans la pensée augustinienne', *Archives de Philosophie* 72 (2009) 249–69.
[14] Cp. Brian Stock, *Augustine's Inner Dialogues: The Philosophical Soliloquy in Late Antiquity*, Cambridge 2010.
[15] The first one, *De pulchro et apto*, has been lost.

similis, and different, *dissimilis*. One example of the difference between the two notions is the difference between knowing God and knowing mathematics. The first is far more attractive than the latter.[16] Why? Because there is a huge difference (*dissimilitudo*) between both kinds of knowledge, the knowledge of God being far more important than any other knowledge. Now, it may look like Augustine is talking about a simple difference, but in fact it is not. In Plato's doctrine, mathematics represents the second-highest phase of knowledge. Mathematics really contain truth and can be conceived of as the last step before entering the realm of absolute truth. In other words, Plato would therefore have insisted on the resemblance between geometrical knowledge and knowledge of the Good. Augustine, however, stresses the fact that we are dealing with a *dissimilitudo*. A genuine difference exists between the highest knowledge and all other knowledge. How does that work out? Well, Augustine in fact uses a highly refined model. At the beginning of the second chapter, he argues that if something looks like something else, it necessarily must be false because it only looks like it.[17] There is only a resemblance to the truth, but things that 'look alike' cannot be true in the real sense of the word. Hence, what is called resemblance can also be called falsehood. It is along these lines of truth and falsehood that he continues to develop his argument. The man you see in your dream is not a true man because he looks like a real man and so on. The conclusion will then be that it is rightly in its similarity with the truth that falsehood finds its shelter: *in veri similitudine habitare falsitatem*.[18] Or, in even more crude terms: *similitudo igitur ... mater est falsitatis*.[19] That is the first step. However, there is something odd in this conclusion: that similarity would be the mother of falsehood. Is this true? In the next passage, Augustine seems to backtrack. The argument runs as follows: if one looks at eggs, is only because eggs resemble one another that we can state that an egg is a true egg. The same goes for a picture of a man. It is convincing because it resembles the real man who is pictured. If this is true, then the

---

[16] *Sol.* I,5,11.
[17] *Sol.* II,6,10.
[18] *Sol.* II,6,12.
[19] *Sol.* II,6,10.

conclusion must *not* be that similarity is the mother of falsehood, but rather that dissimilarity is the mother of falsehood whereas similarity is the mother of truth: *nonne similitudinem veritatis matrem et dissimilitudinem falsitatis esse fatendum est?*[20] This, at least, seems to be a logical conclusion: similarity is the base of the relation with the truth, while dissimilarity is the opposite. However, such a statement is the opposite of the conclusion Augustine had reached some lines earlier, and it can be considered even a reversal of the former position. How, in fact, do we deal with similarity and difference, with true and false? If either statement is right, where can we find some guidance? This is what Augustine wonders with great sighs: *I beg you, please give me the courage to argue that similarity and difference are both responsible for qualifying something as falsehood!*[21]

From there, the two conversationalists reach the next conclusion. There are things that, paradoxically, must be false in order to be true. This means that what is false is not false because it wants to deceive; it is false because it tries to reveal the truth but unfortunately does not manage to do so. Next, if falsehood is indeed the endeavour to reveal the truth, then it must accept its falsehood in order to be credible and to show the truth it wants to reveal. A striking example may be a portrait. A picture of a man must be accepted as a 'false' man in order to truly be the representation it wants to be. An actor must accept that he is not Hector in order to be a credible Hector, a true Hector. This brings the two conversationalists to argue that falsehood can disappear, but the truth cannot for even if one were to say that the truth has died or disappeared, it must be true that the truth has disappeared or died. Truth, therefore, cannot die. Even if she died, it would be true that she has died. Falsehood, therefore, can only be defined as something that is not the truth because it has only a similarity to the truth: *quod a veri similitudine longe abest.*[22] Or, in other words, it is something that is an imitation of the truth.[23] The conversation then continues by expanding on the notion of truth, this time without connecting it any more to the notions of similarity

---

[20]*Sol.* II,7,13.
[21]*Sol.* II,8,15.
[22]*Sol.* II,15,29.
[23]*Sol.* II,16,30.

and difference. First of all, the truth also has its paradoxes. One might argue, for example, that the void, the real nothingness, cannot create its own existence. Nothingness cannot create nothingness. On the other hand, it is called nothingness rightly because it has no relation to the truth. Nevertheless, it exists. How, then, can it be true that something exists which has no relation at all to the truth? It is an oxymoron that recalls the longing of Augustine to discover a truth with no ambivalence in it, and which is not characterized by the dual structure of partial truth and partial falsehood.[24] However, this train of thought concerning the paradoxes of the notion of truth is quickly left aside and both speakers continue to discuss the truth that exits in the field of mathematics. We can indeed find truth in the realm of mathematics, they both agree. Here, then, we are back on the platonic track, contrary to the first chapter of the book: mathematics does carry truth, albeit not in the purest form – and in fact only in a very limited way. However, it is a kind of knowledge that shows us the contours of the truth. How, then? In the following manner: even if we do not entirely remember the truth, there still are elements of the truth that we can discover. Suffice it to think of a man who has lost or forgotten something. His companions will ask him whether it is this, or that, pointing at different objects. He will directly recognize that it was not this or that object he had forgotten. So, even when one has forgotten the object itself, one is still capable of knowing what this object is *not*. There remains some kind of truth, even if we do not see the truth itself. It is on these sorts of reflections that the book ends, at least apparently. As we will soon discover, however, there is another train of thought, which leads to different conclusions from those we have just reached. It is precisely this constant changing of tracks that makes Augustine's writing sometimes difficult to understand. He often seems to elaborate his theme in a rather confusing way, and he certainly does not avoid getting sidetracked. Consequently, his main theme is not always as visible as one might hope. Augustine himself even seems to be aware of the winding roads he takes, as he explicitly mentions the reason why this is a soliloquy: one can only find the truth through a dialogue in which one advances something and

---

[24]*Sol.* II,10,18.

then retracts it.[25] Nevertheless, this fascinating dialogue with one's mind demonstrates that sometimes things are false not because they differ from the truth but because they resemble the truth.

Now what is striking in this whole inner debate is Augustine's extreme longing to reach a truth without ambivalence. As he clearly states, he wants to discover the truth without it being based on a two-sided argumentation (*bifronte ratione*[26]) between similarity and difference. Yet, in the whole book, it has proved impossible to escape from this twofold structure, no matter how much Augustine tried. Indeed, this bifocal structure – which has proved to be omnipresent – is a structure that runs counter to the required simplicity of the truth. But even then, even when it may be out of reach, Augustine wishes to lay hands on such a simple truth, on a truth that is not mixed up with any bifocal structure. He eagerly wants it, and it is this strong desire for a simple truth that is fully approved by his adversary, his Reason. The latter admits that what Augustine is longing for is something great and divine: *magna et divina*. In other words, what Augustine strives for is truth without similarities, and every similarity he comes across can do nothing but negatively affect the truth, even if it is clear that similarity can be the mother of truth. All of this can be understood and the argumentation can even seem correct. What is slightly frightening however – already in this first book of the young Augustine – is the fact that even though similarity has a positive nature, this does not invalidate the fact that it can also be part of falsehood: what is similar must also be dissimilar at the same time. Therefore, there is no avoiding the conclusion that falsehood can be defined in terms of *similarity*, no less than it can in terms of *dissimilarity*. What the future bishop clearly puts forward is that similarity is the mother of falsehood, even if sometimes it is also the mother of truth. Unfortunately, however, he does not seem to take into account this last aspect. Despite his platonic influences, he does not adopt the essential structure of the platonic philosophy; namely the resemblance between the different layers of our reality, which constantly leads us to a higher level. Truth is found thanks to structures of similarity. This is not what Augustine explains in

---

[25] *Sol.* II,7,14.
[26] *Sol.* II,10,18.

this book. On the contrary: similarity has largely lost its positive character. What he emphasizes in this early work is that falsehood can only be called as such because its similarity to the truth reveals its distance to the truth, not only its dissimilarity. This is a particularly negative qualification that leaves us dumbfounded. One might be able to understand that something equals falsehood because of its dissimilarity with the truth; however, according to Augustine, once it has been defined as the consequence of being similar to the truth, everything that carries in it this similarity must also be qualified as falsehood. There is always this *bifronte ratione*. No matter whether we speak about reflection, imitation or image, they all are doomed to be true and false. Notwithstanding their similarity to the truth, they are far away from the truth: there is a huge distance. Admittedly there is indeed a distance between the truth and that which resembles the truth but, in Augustine's view, this distance from now on cannot be separated from falsehood. Perhaps it can be the space of longing or desire, to put it in positive terms, but this desire is immediately caught up in the dynamics of impossibility, inability and failure. Even though Augustine quoted the example of the eggs earlier, he seems to reject it when he comes to his conclusions. Then, there is always this ambiguous nature of our reality. Sure, eggs do resemble one another, and it is because of this resemblance that we call an egg a true egg. The eggs, therefore, allow us, thanks to their mutual resemblance, to discover some parcels of the truth. Unfortunately, all this is apparently of very limited importance. Similarity has also been defined negatively and the possibilities of discovering the truth are therefore strongly reduced.[27] Moreover, this approach is not only the expression of a negative qualification of similarity: it also blurs the difference between similarity and dissimilarity. What we used to call similar has now also become dissimilar, which implies that the epistemological means we possess have become useless. Augustine has pushed back the frontiers of language but, by doing so, he risks reducing language to a structure of words without any sense. Now the consequence is obvious: if this is Augustine's deepest conviction, then theology will never be part of the incarnation and, in fact, it will be a rather poor theoretical exercise. Moreover, even

---

[27]The argument of the eggs is repeated in *De Diu. Q. LXXXIII*, Q. 74.

this theoretical exercise would never correspond to the truth. On the contrary, it would only prove its insufficiency. All this can only be embraced if one supposes that the constant devaluating of the truth by falsehood has a theological background. This background must then be the fact that Augustine wants to maintain the divide between the Creator and the creation, as he emphasizes in the first chapters of the *Soliloquies*.[28] If this divide is indeed an absolute one, then there will never be any truth in the whole of creation that is not at the same time a falsehood. The only real truth can be God, but this truth is deemed unattainable.

Similarity and participation

Perhaps it is for that reason that, unexpectedly, we find another tone of voice amid chapter 2. Augustine explains that subjects can be predicated of predicates that necessarily belong to them.[29] If one thinks of fire, the predicate 'heat' must belong to it and the same goes for snow and white. Such a predicate is called an accident belonging essentially to the subject, so one may conclude: *inest subiecto*, it is in the subject. However, some predicates do not necessarily belong to a subject. A wall can be made of bricks or stones, but neither belongs necessarily to this subject, and these accidents can be considered as separable. The whole argument about inseparable accidents is taken from the *Posterior Analytics* of Aristotle, and Augustine emphasizes that these logical principles are already taught at school. By this he means that this is well known to everyone: these are the principles of normal reasoning. At the end of the second chapter, he returns to this Aristotelian approach and, unexpectedly, radically changes his appreciation of mathematics. Whereas in the first chapter he had mainly insisted on a huge difference between the knowledge of God and the knowledge of mathematics (although mathematics were useful to a certain extent, as we have already seen), he now stresses the fact that there must be truth in mathematics (or, the other way round, that perhaps mathematics belongs to the truth).

---

[28]*Sol.* I,1,2,
[29]*Sol.* II,12,22.

Next, if that is the case with mathematics, the same also goes for our mind (*animus*), as well as for our soul (*anima*).[30] Both possess truth or truth is in them, comparable to the inseparability of a subject. Now, this whole approach is no less than a great reversal of the question as it was treated until now. Augustine alludes to rules of logic defining the relationship between a subject and its accident, and he argues that truth necessarily belongs to the human mind. If this is so, then the whole argument about falsehood seems now to crumble into pieces. We would then have a similarity that leads us to the ultimate truth, and this would overturn the idea that similarity is always characterized by falsehood. Apparently, Augustine suddenly changed his method. What he had done, until now, was to practise an epistemological approach, in which he tried to distinguish between false and true. He now practises an ontological approach that might allow him to look more subtly at the notion of truth. Epistemologically speaking, there was no other possibility than to take for granted (*fac me non metuere!*) that one cannot think about the truth without accepting that the notion of falsehood must be integrated into everything we qualify as true. It is as if we cannot see a radiant blue sky because of dark and thick cloud cover. Ontologically speaking, however, things can be very different. If the mind is capable of distinguishing between true and false, there must be truth in it, or it must participate in the truth. Therefore, truth is an inseparable quality of the mind. Such argumentation could be considered acceptable, but it is difficult to match both approaches with one another.

The only conclusion that seems to be possible is to accept that Augustine simultaneously thinks along different lines and that he did not manage to choose either of the two options. Indeed, it is an inner dialogue we are reading and there are two voices to be heard. The first voice proposes that similarity, taken at face value, seems to offer a positive epistemological approach. Yet, once this notion has been elaborated, it appears that even similarity is a stronghold of falsehood. The second voice takes the opposite stand. It argues that truth belongs to our mind in an inseparable manner, and that connection guarantees the discovery of the ultimate truth. It is the first option in particular that remains an intriguing one.

---

[30] *Sol.* II,19,33.

Not unlike the hidden aspects in Plato's simile of the cave, namely the hidden presence of the shadow, we may suppose that there is a comparable dynamic at work here. Similarity has become the hiding place of dissimilarity and it is for that reason that the notions of similarity and dissimilarity risk losing their specific meaning. However, Augustine does not yet explain why he chose to insist so heavily on dissimilarity. We cannot yet distinguish the real dimensions of this dissimilarity, and therefore we need to elaborate our research on similarity and difference. What is clear, at least, is that the two voices we have heard in the *Soliloquia* seem to have characterized Augustine's thinking for his whole life. Whatever you read of his, there is no escaping the impression that these opposing voices are constantly present. One can certainly hear them in a more moderate form, as Augustine constantly attempts not to lose his grip on the nature of language; he is eager to avoid language becoming senseless. Therefore, there will always be a certain wavering between the platonic approach, in which the positive aspect of the similarity prevails, and other approaches, which emphasize the dissimilarity inside the similarity. It is an aspect one might consider somewhat tragic, but the main question is not about Augustine's personal experiences, about personal tragedy: the main question still concerns the shadow. This is not because of this shadow in itself, but because we cannot understand the dynamics of the notion of the image in our modern culture if we do not manage to identify this dark and hidden side of pagan and Christian thinking.

God as similarity itself: The Trinity and human dissimilarity

How then did Augustine continue after this first work? In fact, he continued mainly by following the second approach, namely the ontological one. He discusses the topic in greater detail in other books such as *De Vera Religione, De Diversis Quaestionibus 83* and his three *Commentaries on Genesis*. In all these books, he insists on the relation between the ultimate good and that which has been derived from this ultimate good and can be considered good only by similarity. We do not find again however, his original doubts about the relationship between similarity and dissimilarity, which refers to the particular fact that these two notions may become blurred once one realizes that similarity always remains imperfect and thus also implies a dissimilarity. At least this is what is seems to be. However, we have already noticed that Augustine shifts from an epistemological approach to an ontological one, when dealing with the terms *similitudo* and *dissimilitudo*. He insists, for example, on the fact that a created nature is subordinated to the nature of the One by whom it was created.[31] This means we are dealing with an ontological inferiority of the creation compared to the Creator. This subordination is suddenly also called *dissimilitudo*, although this term revealed in an earlier phase the epistemological approach. It is this shift to the ontological spectrum that we must study. Why did Augustine do this? Was the epistemological problem too complicated to deal with? The least we can say is that this ontological argument is one of his favourites and it can already be found in his earliest works, such as *De Vera Religione*. In this booklet, he introduces a new element that also appears in many of his other books. The argument runs as follows: something that is true, beautiful or chaste is only true, beautiful or chaste thanks to truth itself, beauty itself and chastity itself. As he puts it in *De Vera Rel.*, truth is the form of everything true and everything can only be true as long as it resembles the truth. Truth, in turn, is nothing other than one of the names of the ultimate Unity,[32] which has a layered structure. This argument, based on comparison and resemblance, is a type of argument Augustine often uses and it runs as a common thread throughout his works.[33] Its structure is quite simple. Everything

---

[31]*De Trin.* XV,16,26: *Quamobrem cum tanta sit nunc in isto aenigmate dissimilitudo dei et verbi dei, in qua tamen nonnulla similitudo comperta est; illud quoque fatendum est, quod etiam cum similes ei erimus, quando videbimus eum sicuti est (quod utique qui dixit, hanc procul dubio quae nunc est dissimilitudinem attendit), nec tunc natura illi erimus aequales. Semper enim natura minor est faciente, quae facta est.*
[32]*De Vera Rel.* XXXVI,66. The example of chastity can be found in *De Diu. Q. LXXXIII*, Q. 23.
[33]*De Trin.* V,10,11; VI,1,2; VI,3,5; VII,1.1.*De Diu. Q. LXXXIII*, Q 23. *De Gen. ad Lit. Imp.* 16,57.

that exists owes its existence to a higher principle, which implies that it can only exist as long as it resembles this higher or highest being. In other words, whether we speak about beauty or chastity, things can only be beautiful or chaste as long as they participate in beauty and chastity themselves. Resemblance, in this ontological sense, is indeed nothing other than participation, which will lead us to the ultimate being – the Principle per se. As such, the argument about resemblance is easy to understand: it is about resemblance and unity and it is purely platonic in its framing.

Now, what happens next is that Augustine extends his argument on resemblance to God Himself. Similarity, or resemblance, is not only a comparative term, an epistemological approach. On the contrary, it also has its own absolute existence, an ontological value. This is the argument he will use in *De Genesi ad Litteram Imperfectus* 16,57–58, stating that God is the similarity in itself.[34] Both elements can be found elsewhere. Not only is all similarity derived from the absolute similarity, but this absolute similarity is nothing other than God himself. Augustine mentions, for example, that the Son has a 'full similarity'[35]: he is the similarity derived from the absolute similarity[36] and that he is not so by participation but, inversely, all things resemble this divine similitude by participation. Another example is the text where he mentions that God is the only one in whom no dissimilarity occurs when it comes to resemblance, and that you could say the Son is generated *from* the Father, but not *by* the Father.[37] Now, this is a new argument that shows an unexpected interpretation of the divinity itself. At first glance, it may seem contradictory, for if God is similarity, similarity in itself remains a notion implying a twofold

---

[34]*De Gen. ad Lit. Imp.* 16,57: *Castitas autem nullius participatione casta est, sed eius participatione sunt casta quaecumque casta sunt. Quae utique in Deo est, ubi est etiam illa sapientia, quae non participando sapiens est, sed cuius participatione sapiens est anima quaecumque sapiens est. Quapropter etiam similitudo Dei, per quam facta sunt omnia, proprie dicitur similitudo; quia non participatione alicuius similitudinis similis est, sed ipsa est prima similitudo, cuius participatione similia sunt, quaecumque per illam fecit deus.*
[35]*De Gen. ad Lit.* I,4,9: *plena similitudine.* Cp. also *De Gen. ad Lit.* 16,58: *Unde intellegitur ita patri esse similem similitudinem suam, ut eius naturam plenissime perfectissimeque impleat.*
[36]*De Diu. Q. LXXXIII,* Q. 23: *Pater, id est iste similitudo, ille cuius similitudo est.*
[37]*De Vera Rel.* XLIII,81.

structure: it is not possible to be similar alone, one must resemble something or someone *else*. It is therefore a notion that is seemingly the opposite of God's divine unity, and it recalls the argument of the third man. However, what makes it acceptable is that we realize that Augustine introduces this absolute similarity in order to anticipate the trinitarian structure of the divinity. This is what he explains in *De Genesi ad Litteram Imperfectus* 16,60. If God resembles someone – and if this resemblance can only be a perfect one – then there is only one solution: namely that God has someone next to Him who is completely His equal and who does not infringe His unity, who must be different, but at the same time identical. Obviously, this can only be the Son of God, and the equality between the Son and the Father, based on perfect similarity, will become one of the main ideas in his trinitarian theology.[38] He thus already puts forward the Christological aspect he will emphasize in *De Trinitate*. This interpretation of similarity is a brilliant stroke and it shows Augustine's refined and sophisticated way of thinking. That is the first aspect, the discovery – thanks to the notion of similarity – of the threeness of the godhead: *iste similitudo, ille cuius similitudo est*.[39] Second, this also leads Augustine to reformulate the relation between similarity and difference, between *similitudo* and *dissimilitudo*. Contrary to his former position in the *Soliloquia*, he now mentions in *De Trinitate*, VII,6,12, that similarity brings us nearer to God, while dissimilarity draws us away from Him.[40] The whole structure of similarity that could not be distinguished from dissimilarity now seems to be smoothed out, at least in this passage. Admittedly, there are also passages in which Augustine clearly depicts the contradiction with which he is struggling. In *De Genesi ad Litteram Imperfectus*, he mentions the absolute similarity between the Father and the Son, but he also mentions that, normally speaking, *dissimilitudo* is part of the *similitudo*. The text is as follows:

> *Regarding then the similarity which represents the Son, there can be no dissimilarity with the One whom He resembles. Yet, because similarities (similia) are different they are the question remains of*

---

[38]*De Gen. ad Lit Imp.* 16,60; *De Trin.* IV,21,32; VII,6,12.
[39]*De Diu. Q. LXXXIII*, Q, 23.
[40]*De Trin.* VII,6,12: *similitudine acceditur ad deum, dissimilitudine receditur ab eo.*

> whether also to some extent dissimilar. However, this particular similarity (similitudo) is not partly different (dissimilis).[41]

The difficulty Augustine struggled with is obvious. On the one hand, he admits that similarity is also a hiding place for dissimilarity, whereas on the other hand, he refuses to apply this principle to the relationship between the Father and the Son. It is then that he can state that the difference between similar and dissimilar has become two separated ways. Dissimilarity no longer belongs to similarity; it has become a different path. Nevertheless, the question remains whether Augustine will stick to his new concept of similarity and dissimilarity, or, feeling the need, will he once again adopt the old scheme of a similarity that is almost the equivalent of dissimilarity? This is at least what seems to become visible once we study the opposite of the divine similarity: the human similarity.

Indeed, there is certainly more. The notion of similarity is not only a notion that refers to a higher level of our reality, allowing us to discover even the trinitarian structure of the godhead. The notion is also used to describe the nature of the incarnation, meaning it describes how God can resemble humans. Indeed, the Son has adopted the nature of human life and, in that sense, He is similar to human beings. Correct, this is the principle of the incarnation; however, this incarnation can only imply a partial similarity between the Son and humans. The Son has effectively adopted the human mortal corporeality, but not its sinful nature.[42] He has become similar to mankind and he adopted the outlook of a man.[43] In other words, He has put down his dissimilarity with mankind and has only become similar to humans. However, this does not concern the sinful nature of mankind.[44] This time, therefore, the

---

[41]*De Gen. ad Lit. Imp.* 16,60: *in illa vero similitudine, quae filius est, non potest quiddam esse dissimilis illi cui simile est. Quoniam similia quaecumque alia sunt, inter se etiam dissimilia ex aliqua parte sunt: ipsa vero similitudo non est ex aliqua parte dissimilis.*
[42]*De Diu. Q. LXXXIII.* Q. 66,6: *Non enim caro peccati erat, quae non de carnali delectatione nata erat, sed tamen inerat in ea similitudo carnis peccati, quia mortalis caro erat. De Gen. ad Litt.* X,18,32: *nec ipsa erat caro peccati, sed similitudo carnis peccati.*
[43]*De Trin.* I,7,14; II,11,20.
[44]*De Trin.* IV,2,4.

similarity is again a partial one, completely following the bare notion of similarity itself: something that is similar is not identical. It is thus obvious that the notion of similarity has a double focus. At the level of the godhead, it allows Augustine to reveal the trinitarian structure of God, but at the ordinary level of human life, similarity remains a notion characterized by great equivocality: it can never be untangled from dissimilarity. The dissimilarity in turn finds its origin apparently in the sinful nature of mankind. Now this is an explanation that can hardly surprise us. If there is anything that might explain why humans cannot be the perfect image of God, and why their similarity is only a partial one, then it must be sin. Sin seems to be the magic word that explains definitely why we cannot live at an equal footing with God and why we have to admit that similarity cannot be conceived of without introducing dissimilarity. Of course, Augustine also mentions mortality as the difference producing the partiality of similarity, but mortality is the result of sin in Augustine's view.[45] Therefore, it would be sin that is the final cause of our defective similarity. The Son of God is the perfect similarity; mankind can never exist in the same way because it has sinned. Even when men will be recreated, this similarity will certainly not entail any equality.[46] But leaving this recreation out of the picture, it is sin that causes our inability to untangle similarity and dissimilarity, and it is precisely this incapacity that demonstrates the everlasting distance between the divine and the human. Augustine has effectively blocked access to the divine by insisting on the fact that every similarity equals a disparity that cannot be overcome. It cannot be overcome because humans are sinners, they will always be sinners, and they are incapable of not sinning. Therefore, we have to deal with the notion of sin in order to more accurately understand how Augustine treats similarity and dissimilarity. This must be a rather lengthy explanation in order to see how Augustine uses the model of participation as an alternative model to the one that makes sin the cause of all dissimilarity.

---

[45] E.g. *De Gen. Ad Litt.* III,21,33; XI,32,42, *Contra Faustum* XIV,3; *De Ciu.* XIII,1 sqq. Augustine deals in detail with the relation sin and death in this book.
[46] *De Trin.* XV,16,26.

About sin

Now, if all were due to sin, we would have found the origin of the shadow. Although Plato did not know the concept of sin, Augustine did, and he made it clear that sin is the reason people will always linger in a state of imperfection and dissimilarity. And, of course, it would explain everything we have been looking for up to now. Moreover, sin is one of the most important notions in Augustine's theology. There is no need to expand on it, but Augustine's theology of grace has constantly moved in the direction of forgiveness of one's sins. Then, in the later phase of his battle against the Pelagians, it also became the theology of predestination, the theology of the perverted will, and finally the theology of the election that had to counter the weight of original sin. All these theological constructs can be considered planets turning around the sun – certainly a dark sun – of sin. Sin is what gives sense to forgiveness and predestination, and in that sense, sin is the theological solution to many existential questions. But in fact, it is a solution to none. It is a dogmatic solution that is far too easy to be acceptable. It is the solution everyone could predict, but which hardly seems to be convincing. Indeed, sin has become the favourite stopgap used by theologians to explain any problem. It has become more than the gift of creation, than the beauty of existence; it is the pervading illness destroying all creational beauty. Is the human will divided? Then it surely must be due to sin. Or is it the other way round, that the divided will undoubtedly push mankind into the direction of sin? Human imperfection? Sin is the cause. Concupiscence? Sin? Envy? And so on. In that sense it is shocking to read how Augustine despises even the beauty of the senses in book X of the *Confessions*; it is all sin. It is indeed a theme he does not want to avoid and so he focuses on related themes such as guilt, forgiveness and grace. Yet all these books and treatises have only led to interpretations that fit easily into a dogmatic schema: creation, fall, grace, redemption and eventually election. It is therefore inevitable that sin is a major theme in the *Confessions*, which rightly has to be understood as a pun on a double meaning of *confession* (sin and confession of faith).[47]

---

[47]Though a recent French translation calls the book *Les Aveux* (What has to be admitted), which is not necessarily related to sin. Cp. Frédéric Boyer, *Saint Augustin, Les Aveux*, Paris 2008.

Yet the whole discourse on sin does not explain how we can interpret the relationship between similarity and dissimilarity. One might compare sin to dissimilarity but, in that case, the positive alternative is lacking. One cannot really suggest 'grace' is the positive side of the coin. Grace is not at all the automatic complement of sin. It is utterly contingent, and far from being something one can count on. If one could count on it, runs Augustine's argument, it would no longer be grace but it a kind of due. Therefore, sin cannot be compared to dissimilarity because it does not have a complement comparable to similarity reflecting dissimilarity. Beauty goes with ugliness, virtue with vice, day with night. But sin has no complement; it is an absolute ruler. It can only be compared to a black hole in which all the light of the universe disappears. Indeed, it is a dark sun, a black hole. Once sin has entered the scene, it behaves like a Hydra: whatever head may be chopped off, there are always two more heads to replace the former. Of course, sin can be denied, but in that case, it is not explained. Well, if that is correct and if sin has become such an important notion in Christianity, from where does this emphasis come? In other words, why has sin become such a powerful notion, while the same word in Greek literature, *hamartia*, has never gained a comparable importance in Greek thinking[48]? How did sin manage to become so important, and how did it gain such an overwhelming influence? Without going too deeply into details, one might observe that sin is a moral concept as well as a religious one. However, these aspects in and of themselves are not necessarily harmful. What is harmful, though, is the fact that sin has become a central theme in Christian dogmatics, and that it has become a dominating aspect in the relationship between God and men. How did this happen?

Let us start with the observation that 'sin' is a notion that takes utterly serious the fact that mankind is fallible and, morally speaking,

---

[48]Cp. Ronald Paulson, *Sin and Evil: Moral Values in Literature*, Yale 2007; Marguerite Shuster, *The Fall and Sin: What We Have Become as Sinners*, Grand Rapids 2004; Gary A. Anderson, *Sin: A History*, Yale 2009. Though Laela Zwollo in her excellent book speaks about the relationship between the Augustinian notion of sin and the Plotinian one, I am not convinced at all that Plotinus' ideas on the harmful tendencies the soul may pursue do resemble the Christian notion of sin. Cp. Laela Zwollo, *St Augustine and Plotinus: The Human Mind as Image of the Divine*, Leiden/Boston 2018, 175–8.

extremely vulnerable. Indeed, we sometimes act in a way that morally speaking is unimaginable and sin, in this case, is the notion that exposes this unacceptable behaviour. Hence, sin taken as a notion symbolizing mankind's moral fragility would be understandable. It would be the antidote to a kind of boundless optimism about mankind's nature, about our possibilities to improve life, to improve our behaviour, and even to improve our societal life. It would be the antidote to the perfectionism that pervades our societies – to the point where, even at the time of the current Covid-19 crisis, the main implication is that one should never waste a good crisis. In other words, even during a crisis, one is expected to perform almost flawlessly. It is for this reason that theologians underline the importance of the notion of sin: it is the necessary opposite to modern optimism about human capacities and moral behaviour. What theologians put forward, therefore, is that sin is the only notion that fathoms the hidden parts of our nature. Once again, in that sense sin can be a notion worth the trouble. This is exactly what Augustine highlights when he objects, against the Pelagians, that man's will is not something on which one can count. On the contrary, the human will is divided and if one does not take into account this inner divide, one might fall into the trap of naïve optimism and harmful perfectionism. That is Augustine's opinion at least since his *Ad Simplicianum*, although scholars disagree on whether this Augustinian stance implies continuity or discontinuity in his thinking.[49] Besides, this idea of human fragility is certainly not Christian in its origin. While Augustine often refers to Romans 7,15–16, it was Ovid who had already articulated it in his *Metamorphoses*, saying, 'I see the right and I approve it too, I condemn the wrong and yet the wrong pursue'.[50] Hence, this idea can

---

[49]In fact, Augustine changed his views on the possibilities of the human will, which is quite visible in his book *De Libero Arbitrio*, where the radical change produces a shift between book III on the one hand and the earlier books I and II on the other hand. For a recent overview and an analysis of Augustine's works with regard to free will, see Kenneth M. Wilson, *Augustine's Conversion from Traditional Free Choice to 'Non-Free Will': A Comprehensive Methodology*, Tübingen 2018. See also Michael Frede, *A Free Will: Origins of the Notion in Ancient Thought*, Berkeley 2011.

[50]Ovid, *Metamorphoses* VII,20: *video meliora proboque, deteriora sequor*. A well-known quote, but Ovid already hints at this fragility in the preceding lines.

be considered a classical *topos*: the human will is not to be counted on. Free will, in Augustine's view, is only possible once men are gifted with divine grace; otherwise, the human will is deemed defective and divided. He expanded on this theme in *Confessions*, where he insisted on the contradictions of the human will.[51] Of course, the Manichaeans explained away this phenomenon by arguing that these were the two natures found in the human mind: one good, the other bad. But Augustine had long since set aside this 'solution'. Divine grace is meant to 'cure' humanity's imperfections, due to his sinful nature. This is the recurrent theme in his battle against the Pelagians: that the human will is not capable of living up to its own standards. It wills something but at the same time, it wills something else, something that is the opposite of what it had originally willed. What Augustine is therefore aiming for is to clarify that any naïve optimism about the capacities of human nature may lead us astray from the reality of a broken human existence. One might argue that Augustine is certainly right in emphasizing human fragility and the different directions our will can take; it is true that the will, to be will, must have a contingent character – for there was only one option, what would be left for our will to will?[52]

The notion of sin can certainly be a useful reminder of human weakness. Nonetheless, the way it has been framed in Christianity ensures that it is an unacceptable notion. The argument runs as follows: the defective nature of mankind cannot be attributed to God, first of all. That is an understandable starting point, but it results in an obligation to picture a coherent composition of contrasting notions such as creation, freedom, failure, obedience and love. For if God is not the ultimate cause of all that is contained in creation, what then is the reason for the tragedy of human imperfection? Is it not true that, somewhere in the narrative, notions such as imperfection, fall and disobedience must be brought in, although admittedly, we do not understand how these notions can be related to a perfect creation created by a perfect God? If this perfect creation produces imperfect and morally reprehensible acts, how

---

[51] *Conf.* VIII,10,23–4.
[52] Yet, even in his *De Lib Arb.*, Augustine does not expand on this aspect of contingency.

can this have happened without God's involvement? That, at least, is the red line theologians had never crossed since Manichaeism was rejected. There is only one God, and He cannot be the origin of evil nor of imperfection.[53] This was also the Neoplatonist stance, but Neoplatonism was able to explain that once the One had produced emanations, these emanations could only be less perfect than the One itself. This was already visible once you realized that every emanation belonged to the reign of multiple beings and could no longer be considered as 'one' and single. It is in that sense that Plotinus also speaks of 'forgetting' the One.[54] However, this model could not be adopted by Christianity as it rejected the idea of emanations and replaced it with the model of creation.[55] The creation, however, was the product of a good and perfect Creator and hence there was no explanation available for everything that proved to be less than perfect. There was only the notion of a divide between Creator and creation, which in itself was not necessarily considered to be an absolute one. The well-known doctrine of deification, developed in the East, was the proof of a kind of possible bridge between God and man. However, once this gap was filled, not with notions such as deification but with an insurmountable notion of hereditary sin, the divide became absolute. Augustine struggles with these complex questions in book VII of his *Confessions*, and traces the well-known features of what will become the solution of Western Christianity, namely that all is the fault of man – something he will pursue in *De*

---

[53] Cp. *Sol.* I,1,2,: *deus qui malum non facis*.

[54] Cp. *Enn.* VI,I,1. Cf also *Enn.* III,8 and VI,8. Laela Zwollo, in her very instructive work on the augustinian image, speaks of 'similarities to Plotinus's Doctrine of Sin on the basis of *Enn.* V,1.1 and the use of the word τόλμα. However, Plotinus does not speak of sin, he only explains why we forget the One. The reason of this oblivion is the will to have a proper existence and in that sense his picture of the will comes closer to the idea of hubris than that of sin. Cp. Laela Zwollo, *St. Augustine and Plotinus: The Human Mind as Image of the Divine*, Leiden 2019, 175–8. In *Enn.* III,2,10 on the contrary, he speaks of *hamartia*, but this cannot be compared to the Christian notion of sin.

[55] Though Augustine sometimes seems to refer to a more Neoplatonist model, e.g. in *Conf.* X,29,40 where he writes: *Per continentiam quippe colligimur et redigimur in unum, a quo in multa defluximus*. The wording here is completely grafted on Neoplatonist models and has very little to do with the notions of Creator and creation.

Genesi ad Litteram. There, he insists on the hereditary nature of sin, basing himself on a wrong translation of Romans 5,12, the famous question of the *in quo omnes peccaverunt*. At least then, the moral fragility of man cannot be attributed to God, who is perfect and can never be the source or origin of imperfection. There is no other option than to blame man for the introduction of imperfection, in particular moral imperfection, and this moral imperfection is qualified as trespassing the divine commandments — a transgression called sin.[56] The argument is a shaky one as it does not explain from where this sin originated,[57] but rather serves to deny any divine responsibility in the history of sin.[58] In other words, mankind is accused and sacrificed to preserve the divine Goodness, which is exactly the opposite of the other Christian paradigm of a God sacrificing Himself for the benefit of men. Subsequently, sin is not only considered to describe human fallibility but also to express outrage against God. This outrage then produces unforgivable guilt that can only be paid for by redemption. To sum up: on the one hand it is not clear why sin cannot be related to the Creator, while on the other hand it creates an unforgivable debt that man owes God. Humans are therefore trapped in a system without any possible escape. You are doomed to fail, but this remains your responsibility, even though it is impossible not to sin. It is a blatant reversal of what happens: the sacrifice of man in order to protect an innocent God. Since then, the story of mankind no longer starts with divine love, with community, but starts with sin and ends with it as in a

---

[56] As Augustine puts it very shortly in *Conf.* X,4,5: my good deeds are in fact your good deeds, my faults are exclusively mine: *Bona mea instituta tua sunt et dona tua, mala mea delicta mea sunt et iudicia tua*.

[57] Augustine admits this explicitly in *De Lib. Arb.* II,20,54: *Unde igitur erit (sc. voluntas cum se avertit ab incommutabili bono ad mutabile bonum) Ita quaerenti tibi, si respondeam nescire me, fortasse eris tristior: sed tamen vera responderim*. And in *De Ciu* XII,7, he explains that indeed there is no *causa efficiens* for this *mala voluntas*. There is only a *causa deficiens*. If there would be a *causa efficiens*, there would be something that precedes the will, which is not the case. There, there can only be a causa deficiens.

[58] It is of course the difficult question of the theodicy, that occupied Augustine very much. Cp. Johannes Brachtendorf, 'The Goodness of Creation and the Reality of Evil. Suffering as a Problem in Augustine's Theodicy', *Augustinian Studies* 31(2000) 79–92.

kind of eternal inclusion. Moreover, the principle of justice has been abolished. Justice is no longer a matter of pursuing the good and punishing what is evil, it only serves to justify a relationship that, in itself, is already the reversal of justice. This makes it impossible to speak of moral behaviour in a meaningful way because the dogmatic framework has already decided that man is a morally destroyed being. This applies even more once sin becomes definitely associated with sexuality, and once sexuality has become an exclusive domain of sinful desire,[59] dubbed 'concupiscence'.[60] Concupiscence will be the nightmare with which Augustine had to fight his whole life, which caused him to distrust even the gifs of the senses, like the pleasure of colours, fragrances, music.[61] Concupiscence, the divided will: these were the battlefields Augustine created in his fight with the Pelagians, which they unsurprisingly lost. It was not about perfectionism, it was not about grace, it was about the possibility to think of mankind in terms other than those of a morally spoilt being. Sin, therefore, is an essential part of the history of a play without a script.

Now, this whole argumentation about sin is a rather perverse way of looking at human imperfection. It is very much unlike the era of the Greek tragedy, ranging from the fifth century BC to Late Antiquity, where we encounter the same picture of human imperfection. However, when it comes to *hamartia*, Greek tragedy tries to understand what happens and refrains from judging too quickly.[62] It insists on our lack of understanding. We do not understand why others behave as they do, but neither do we understand our own doings. In other words, there is a lack of understanding due to our

---

[59]In a very instructive article, James Wetzel insists on this aspect of desire and Augustine's continuous struggle with it: James Wetzel, 'Augustine on the Will', in Mark Vessey, ed., *A Companion to Augustine*, Oxford 2012, 339–52.
[60]It is one of the modern objections against Augustine, coming from a feminist point of view. E.g. Cp. Judith Chelius Stark, *Feminist Interpretations of Augustine*, Pennsylvania 2007. Virginia Burrus, Mark D. Jordan and Karmen Mackendrick, *Seducing Augustine: Bodies, Desires, Confessions*, New York 2010. Of course, the most detailed study on body and sexuality remains P. Brown, *The Body and Society: Men, Women, and Sexual Renunciation in Early Christianity*, New York 1988.
[61]Cp. *Conf.* X,31,47–34,53.
[62]Cp. Kyle Harper, *From Shame to Sin: the Christian Transformation of Sexual Morality in Late Antiquity*, Harvard 2013.

blindness to our own constitution. What happens to human beings is that they may be too quick to judge, too stubborn to recognize, too eager to act and so on. However, that is at the level of acts. At the level of moral understanding (and this seems to me even more important), Greek tragedy insists on the ardent desire of humans to act as morally responsible beings. Unfortunately, it is precisely this moral approach that confronts humans with their inability to deal with moral duties once these duties seem to be contradictory. It is a conflict in which one tries to behave according to certain values, but it is precisely these values and the desire to respect them leads paradoxically to morally unacceptable behaviour. This is the blindness by which humans live, and which Oedipus fully recognizes, in *Oedipus Rex*, albeit only at the end. This is such a frightful discovery, however, that one may prefer to no longer see what one sees. A great tragedy and deception lingers in the fact that moral behaviour produces immoral behaviour. Hence, Oedipus inflicts upon himself the blindness he had lived by, as long as he had tried to behave as responsibly as possible. Of course Fate seems to play a role, but Fate is not an objective cause, a kind of cosmic watch counting down without mercy until the catastrophe happens. It is rather the idea that our nature hides unknown miracles and cruelties, a kind of *akrasia*, which we only discover once our moral obligations seem to contradict each other. Beware therefore of any rationalism that suggests people can always act rationally and responsibly. The irrational side of our behaviour, once we are confronted with different duties, is much more important than we normally consider it to be. That, at least, was one of the lessons Euripides left us in his tragedies, such as the *Bacchae*, *Hyppolitus* and *Hecuba*. Now, then, is this blindness comparable to the notion of sin or is it not? Is it something that belongs to human nature in the same way that heredity marks our existence? In short, is it justifiable to sharply distinguish between committing inevitable moral failures and sin that clings to our existence as a congenital defect? Well, in my view, it is reasonable to distinguish between both approaches of human nature. The Greek notion of failure is a human affair in which the gods have very little to do. It is even worse: they can behave like human beings and their behaviour is no less exposed to moral contradictions. That is the reason even the gods can be accused of immoral behaviour; indeed, their acts are far from being beyond any criticism and that is why they can be held accountable. This is far from comparable to a system in which God not only enacts solid moral laws but also creates the conditions for trespassing them. The divine law is created by God in order to be obeyed, but humans are created in such a way that they have to obey their nature, which is to trespass. It is this trap that is completely different from the notion of 'the fragility of goodness' in the famous words of Martha Nussbaum.[63] It is the acceptance of the paradoxical aspect of our existence that turns our moral outlook upside down. Hecuba ends up as a kind of horrifying dog and will, in the end, be transformed into solid rock amid the seas, a rock causing shipwrecks and disasters:

> *If we could not be turned into dogs, we would no longer be humans. And a question linking tragedy and philosophy in this culture, as all these works have in their different ways seen, is whether, and how, that dog's rock is to be allowed to stand in our world. Whether we want an ethical conception that puts an end to these problems, or whether we wish to be left where we began, as characters in a tragedy. Whether we want an art of thought, and also of writing, that engenders, and embodies, fixity and stability, or an art that encourages our souls to remain plantlike and fragile, places of glancing light and flowing water.*[64]

Sin, in contrast to the Greek *hamartia*, will never be defined with the notion that if we could not sin, we would not be humans. On the contrary, sin will always be something to avoid, something that denatures the divine image we still possess in our inner being. Its function is therefore completely different from that of the Greek *hamartia*. It does not stress the moral conflicts we may struggle with, but it focuses on the need for protecting the goodness and the inviolability of the divinity. It is for this reason one might put forward that the notion of sin can be seen as a rational solution for an unsolvable mystery. Who is to blame for the moral errors that humans commit? It cannot be the deity; it therefore must be mankind. What can mankind be reproached with? Trespassing – which is nothing other than sinning. We can therefore reach the

---

[63] Martha Nussbaum, *The Fragility of Goodness*, New York 2001.
[64] Martha Nussbaum, *op.cit.* 421.

following conclusion: although sin in itself may be irrational, it explains in a rational way why something went wrong, and who is to blame. The reasons for the sin of Adam and Eve may be completely incomprehensible, but the fact that they sinned explains why humans behave as they do. Sin is, therefore, a rational element in an otherwise irrational system. It explains failure and guilt, but it also protects the deity from accusations. This means that the distance between humans and the divine becomes an unbridgeable one, and it is especially in this sense that Augustine seems to use sin. The only 'bridge' available is grace but grace can only be bestowed by God, implying that the bridge remains one-way traffic. This is how notions such as sin, grace, freedom, will, nature have become corrupted and remain, in Augustine's theology, concepts that result in sacrificing mankind in favour of a God who will pretend that it is precisely the other way round. In the end, the notion of sin, though rationally understandable, is a poor and pitiful concept. It is a caricature of human nature; it is, theologically, speaking a stopgap and has nothing to do with a mature reflection on human nature. It has made it impossible to consider human beings as multilayered in nature; it has reduced human nature to a one-dimensional phenomenon.[65] Of course, this also had some devastating consequences for the doctrine of atonement. Atonement is one of the most difficult, albeit necessary, acts in human life. One could therefore consider God as the source of all atonement, as the force enabling us to achieve atonement between humans. However, due to the doctrine of sin and salvation, atonement has become the act only God can achieve, and it considers the atonement between God and men. This has been fleshed out in later centuries by Anselm, who developed the classical doctrine of atonement, but this doctrine was originally built on the notion of sin and salvation that was developed in early Christianity, not least by Augustine.

---

[65]One might point at the book of Kurt Flasch, *Logik des Schreckens. Augustinus von Hippo: Die Gnadenlehre von 397*, Mainz 1990. Flasche's picture however is merely black and white though the most fascinating question is to discover how Augustine maintains both strands of thought and how me moves from one shore to the other.

4

The different forms of similarity

There is another tone of voice in Augustine's work, however – barely audible at points – which is not about sin but about similarity and dissimilarity. There, we seem to be much nearer to the Greek approach, where there is something that suddenly changes its appearance and becomes the opposite of what it was. There is a moral standard but, as soon as one tries to realize it, it turns into its opposite. Indeed, there is similarity but the more we recognize similarity, the more we have to acknowledge an inherent dissimilarity. Here we find the other tone of voice in which sin has not the central place it occupies in other parts of Augustine's theology. It is this tone of voice that is fascinating. Of course, we can still accept that sin is the ultimate answer to our question regarding the shadow present in this life. But then we will have forgotten about Augustine's subtle, though clearly present, thoughts on explanations other than those related to sin. As such we do not want to stop at the level of sin, which in fact is an admission of weakness; we will try to find the answer in domains other than that of sin. What is required, therefore, is a further analysis of the similarity that can make this tone of voice more audible, showing us another way of interpreting the dark side of our existence. Such voices can be heard in Augustine's three commentaries on the first lines of Genesis, as well as in *De Ciuitate dei*.

At first glance, these books do not provide new perspectives on the notion of similarity. What Augustine remarks in *De Genesi contra Manichaeos* is that the Manicheans reject the idea of man as created in the likeness and image of God. In their view, this would imply that God has a corporeal outlook. Men have a body and, if they have been created according to God's image, then God must also have a body – something Augustine considers ridiculous. First of all, when speaking about God, it goes without saying that one has to use metaphorical language. Hence, whenever one speaks of God's feet or eyes, these can be nothing other than metaphorical eyes and feet. Such is the case in the Old and New Testaments. More important, however, is the fact that after the first lines in Genesis 1 (*let us create men according to our image and similarity*), God continues by saying '*so that they may rule over the fish in the sea and the birds in the sky, over the livestock and all the wild animals, and all the creatures that move along the ground according to their kinds*'. In other words, being created in the image of God means to have power over all the animals.[1] The divine image humans possess must be conceived of as a kind of representation of the creator and it has nothing to do with any corporeal outlook. Moreover, this power can even be interpreted metaphorically. If humans are able to rule over all the animals, one could also understand that this might imply the animal in man himself, namely his 'animal instincts'. These instincts should be dominated no less than the real animals.[2] Finally, it must be clear that mankind is created as a mixture of body and soul, and of course it is only the soul that is created in the image of God.[3] That is the way Augustine explains the creation of man according to God's image in *De Genesi ad Litteram* III. It is in these chapters that he expands on the image and where he insists on its incorporeal aspect, revealing that it can only be the soul or mind[4] that is created as God's image and/or according to His image.[5] The body, on the contrary, was created by God shaping a human being with clay, with this rough material. In this case, the body is certainly not what represents the similarity with God. Moreover, it is only kept together by the soul, just as clay is held together by water.[6] However, Augustine is still concerned

---

[1] *De Gen. contra Man.* I,17,27–28.
[2] *De Gen. contra Man.* I, 20,31.
[3] *De Gen. ad Litt.* VII,22,32: *Faciamus hominem ad imaginem et similitudinem nostram (quod nisi secundum animam recte intellegi non potest).*
[4] Augustine speaks of *ratio vel mens vel intellegentia*, *De Gen. ad Litt.* III,20,30.
[5] Cp. *De Gen. ad Litt.* III,20,30.
[6] *De Gen. contra Man.* II,7,9.

about the body and does not want to condemn it entirely. The body itself, he explains in *De ciuitate dei XIV*, is not evil. It is the soul that started to sin by not obeying God's commandments, and this disobedience of course affected the body; the body in itself is not in any sense the equivalent of evil. Yet from the moment the soul sinned, the body was drawn in the same direction and it started to suffer from passions, in particular the four classical passions: desire, fear, joy and sorrow.[7] It participates in the sinning that the soul had committed, because body and soul are a unity. Hence the decay of the body can only be the result of the original sin. The decay of the body, indulging in the passions, is not the origin of sin; it is the punishment for human disobedience. It is this 'carnal' aspect that drove Augustine to distinguish in *De ciuitate dei* the *carnal* city from the *spiritual* one: the latter as the city in which humans live in peace, the former as the city of arms and different languages.[8] Although there is, according to St Paul, certainly a difference between the flesh and the body, the shift from the one to the other remains confusing in this case. The word 'carnal' in the carnal city is linked to a Pauline heritage, but it does no justice at all to the subtle distinction Augustine had precisely introduced between a body that in itself does not represent sin, but is drawn in the direction of evil by the soul. Indeed it was not the body, but rather the soul (meaning the spirit), and hence the body became almost the equivalent of the flesh. Logically speaking, then, it would have been preferable to speak more positively about the 'carnal' city but, unfortunately, Augustine succumbed to the pressure of Pauline theology.[9] In doing so, he contributed to the condemnation of the body that, for centuries, has been so present in our culture and that now turns into its opposite – which of course is something different from accusing Augustine of having created this tradition! He did not; he followed a tradition that was stronger than his own argumentation.

However, all this can hardly be surprising. Of course the similarity between God and man is not founded on corporeality. Augustine

---

[7] *De Ciu.* XIV,3,2.
[8] *De Ciu.* XIV,1.
[9] Cp. Andrea Nightingale, 'Appendix, Augustine on Paul's Conception of the Flesh and the Body', in, Andrea Nightingale ed., *Once out of Nature: Augustine on Time and the Body*, Chicago 2011, 211–18.

insists that similarity is the result of the creational act of God: God created man in His image and likeness. This is what he constantly repeats in his books on the first chapters of Genesis. The formulation has to be taken very seriously: man is not created *as* the image of God, but *according to* the image of God. The argumentation he develops runs as follows: looking at the first verses of Genesis, we come across the creation of plants and fruits, of which Augustine states that they are created according to their nature and resemblance: *secundum suum genus et similitudinem*.[10] This is an important observation. These plants do not resemble anything else; they have been created according to their nature (*genus*), so there is an existence in which similarity concerns only one's own nature. A plant must obey the rules of its own nature. This is an additional remark to the previous verses, where this observation was absent, because plants and fruits have their own offspring contrary to heaven and earth. Therefore, the reason this similarity is now added is that the fruit of a tree must give birth to a tree that resembles the tree from which it is the offspring.[11] However, nothing is mentioned about the nature of this similarity, and dissimilarity does not seem to play any role at all. The picture changes later in the book when Augustine expands on the creation of man. He differentiates between similarity and image, arguing that similarity is not always the same as image. For example, two trees may bear a certain resemblance without being the image one of another.[12] Being an image of something implies that an original exists, but man is not just the image of the original: he is only created according to the image. If that is the case, then it should also be added that he is created according to the likeness of God because God is likeness itself, as we have already seen. All other things are something by participation. One is chaste by participating in chastity itself, and those we call wise participate in wisdom. This is something Augustine had already mentioned in his interpretation of the enlightened nature of the human mind: such a mind participates in the eternal light.[13] Now, the introduction in

---

[10] *De Gen. c. Man.* I,13,19; II,11,34; II,13,39. *De Gen. ad Litt* II,12,25; III,12,19; V,4,9.
[11] *De Gen. c. Man.* II,13,19.
[12] *De Gen. Imp.* 16,57.
[13] *De Gen. ad Litt.* III,20,31: *particeps aeternae atque incommutabilis sapientiae dei.*

this paragraph of the notion of *participation* is a critical one. We are back again in the sphere of platonic philosophy in which reality is always multilayered, where the lower parts are participating in the higher ones. Moreover, if the model of a platonic worldview is adopted once again, it will no longer be possible to maintain that the lower parts are only created *according* to a likeness: they must be likenesses themselves. This means that man is not only created according to the image of God, he also *is* the image of God. That, however, is a huge step. A step, nevertheless, that Augustine will take.[14]

Nevertheless, it is clear that, within this model, there is no longer room for the notion of falsehood. The only possibility left to distinguish between the image and its original is the notion of inequality.[15] Something can resemble something else to a larger or a minor degree; it can even be a perfect image and therefore possess the quality of equality, but it cannot be false or true. At least not in the way something is false or true within the Creator-creature divide. If the creation and the creatures are radically different from the Creator, and if this gulf cannot be bridged, then the model of participation is not applicable. Until now, Augustine was able to speak of falsehood because he wanted to maintain this absolute divide. However, once he introduces the model of participation, this whole argumentation loses its validity. Augustine is aware of this shift and of the huge steps he is taking. At the end of this unfinished book, he still doubts and cannot decide whether to opt for man created as an image or for man as created according to the divine image. Therefore, he hesitantly argues that indeed man is an image of God, but that this image is made according to the image of God: *Est tamen et homo imago Dei ... Sed haec imago ad imaginem Dei facta.*[16] The difference between the Son – who is the real and absolute image of the Father – and man is the fact that there is no equality between God and man[17] and hence there is a dissimilarity,

---

[14]A first step is already taken in *De Gen. ad Litt.* III,22,34 where Augustine explains that only the mind can be called God's image. Cp also III,24,37; VI,7,12; XII,7,18.
[15]Cp. *De Trin.* IX,2,2: *impari imagine, sed tamen imagine*. X,12,19: *altissimam essentiam cuius impar imago est humana mens*. Also XV,23,43.
[16]*De Gen. Imp.* 16,61.
[17]Augustine repeats that man as a divine image is *impar* compared to God. Cf. *De Trin.* VII,6,12; XV,23,43.

which does not apply to the case of the Son. Even if man had not sinned, even then he would not be identified with the perfect image, which is the Son.[18]

The Augustinian ambivalence

A hesitant Augustine: this is what strikes the reader. Where will Augustine finally end up? His argumentation may indeed be difficult to trace, but at least it is clear that he uses different types of argumentation and that suddenly one type can be put aside in favour of another. This may seem a wild goose chase: where is the real Augustine hiding, and what does he really think about falsehood? The three books on Genesis do not help us to move forward. They introduce once again the notion of participation we have already come across, but the notion of similarity is not analysed in a more detailed way. Indeed, the notion is frequently used in book XII of *De Genesi ad Litteram*, but there it concerns corporeal images and their resemblances to spiritual realities. It is indeed a very winding road Augustine traces in his book. Is he focusing on the platonic model of resemblance and participation that excludes to a large extent the notion of falsehood? Or does he finally prefer the idea of the unbridgeable divide between the Creator and creation? This what seems to be the case in his last book of *De Trinitate*. There, finally, the notion of dissimilarity recurs, ending with the same conclusion we have already come across in the *Soliloquies*. What is Augustine's argument? First of all, he starts by insisting on the fact that our words cannot resemble the Word of God. This divine Word has become flesh, sure, but this does not mean that it has transformed itself into flesh (*mutaretur in carnem*). It has only adopted this flesh;[19] it has certainly not assumed the flesh (*non in eam se consumendo*[20]) – which by the way is an incredibly limited way of conceiving the incarnation. However, the more our human words become interiorized as parts of our souls, the more they will

---

[18]*De Gen. Imp.* 16,61.
[19]*De Trin.* XV,11,20.
[20]*De Trin.* XV,11,20. Cp also XV,11,21; XV,16,26.

reflect true knowledge and the more they will look like the divine Word. Hence there will be a similarity, but only a limited one: the difference between the two kinds of words being primordial. Augustine keeps insisting on the essential difference between the divine Word and human ones, basing himself on the divide between the Creator and the creation. In other words, we are back in the realm of the *dissimimilitudo*, establishing that human words are very much unlike the divine one. So, once again, the notions of similarity and dissimilarity are linked one to another. Augustine then argues, in *De Trinitate* XV,16,26, that once we will be similar to God, indeed, but that it is precisely this similarity that reveals that we are very much unlike God.[21] This time, however, he takes care not to call this dissimilarity 'falsehood'. No, human words are certainly not false because they do not lie or err. Nevertheless, they are certainly nothing more than swirling elements, turning from one topic to another. His conclusion, therefore, leaves no doubt: although human capacities may represent the image that reflects the divine Trinity, we should be cautious about comparing it to this divine Trinity. There is indeed a resemblance (*similitudo*) but inside this resemblance there is a great dissimilitude: *sed potius in qualicumque ista similitudine magnam quoque dissimilitudinem cernat*,[22] which is the conclusion he repeats several times.

There we are then. Twenty-five years after the *Soliloquies*, the conclusion remains the same in almost the same terms. A conclusion that Augustine only discloses in the last book of *De Trinitate*. Apparently, he did not want to interrupt the argumentation of the previous books in which he insisted on the resemblance between the human image and its divine origin. In the latter books, he expanded largely on the notion of participation and seemingly wanted to demonstrate that the kinship between God and man can never be lost. That is at least what he says in book XIV,8,11: even if the image no longer participates in God, it still remains God's image.[23] Augustine therefore maintains this view until the very last book of *De Trinitate* and it is only in book XV that the argumentation

---

[21]*De Trin.* XV,16,26: *hanc procul dubio quae nunc est dissimilitudinem attendit.*
[22]*De Trin.* XV,20,39.
[23]*Diximus enim eam etsi amissa dei participatione obsoletam atque deformem, dei tamen imaginem permanere.*

suddenly collapsed. The whole argument of the previous books is swept aside: the idea that memory and participation are so strongly connected one to another that it is impossible that the divine image, possessed by man, should disappear. This platonic model, which prevailed in the second half of *De Trinitate* and which is completely contrary to the idea of any dissimilarity, is left behind. We will return to these books once we have examined the notion of memory. However, we can already mention that the picture falters in the XVth book. It is not participation that is the stairway to identification with the divine reality; it is once again dissimilarity that must be emphasized. This may shock the reader in a way; *De Trinitate* is a book in which Augustine gradually reveals how solid the kinship between God and man still is, even after the Fall. Yet suddenly and unexpectedly the ancient motive of incompatibility pops up again, and without warning. Augustine indeed hesitated, but ultimately decided to put all his eggs in one basket, so to speak. This seems to be the final conclusion: dissimilarity will always prevail. Firstly, there is of course great dissimilarity between a man who is the image of God and God who is the creator of this image. Even after the resurrection, this image remains a partial one. God will be seen as He is, but man as his image will never attain any equality with God. This implies that indeed, on the epistemological side, there will be correct knowledge that no longer has anything to do with falsehood. However, at an ontological level, there will be no equality. That seems to be the final conclusion of Augustine. He needed both models: the model that will provide him with the perspective of full knowledge, based on participation that will increasingly bring the image nearer to its origin; and a model that maintains the divide between Creator and creation. Yet, although Augustine opted for this divide, it is this particular choice that leaves our main question unanswered: what is the very nature of this dissimilarity? We have left sin aside but, by doing so, the question remains a pressing one. How can we explain that, apart from sin, there is a dissimilarity inside each similarity that completely undermines this similarity? It is like a fire: one can appreciate its warmth, but the heat of the fire cannot be separated from its possible destructive nature. This means that the real danger of this dissimilarity has to be situated in the possible presence of evil. On the whole, there is a kind of counterforce that has installed itself in this dissimilarity, yet it is hardly identifiable.

This is more than a simple conclusion based on clear evidence from Augustine's books; it is also a deplorable conclusion, revealing Augustine's strong desire to turn a blind eye to the moral ambiguities he himself created. Augustine apparently refuses to identify the moral swamp in which humans can drown, the dissimilarity we cannot identify. He watches the moral disarray in which humans find themselves, but the only solution he proposes is to reveal that they have sinned, and that they necessarily will continue to do so, because sin has become the original sin that cannot be avoided. If sin were the only reason, however, then both of the models adopted by Augustine would be difficult to harmonize with his hamartiology. The epistemological model explains that it is impossible to leave aside the notion of falsehood once we speak about truth. But can falsehood and truth in an epistemological sense be equal to sin and sinlessness? One might think so, for Augustine seems to suggest that dissimilarity relates to sin. However, this argumentation will not fly. Dissimilarity must be situated inside similarity: once you have something that is similar, Augustine insisted that it is at the same time dissimilar. But sin is not a necessary part of impeccability; one cannot pretend that once one conceives impeccability, sin must necessarily be incorporated in this notion. On the contrary, sin is the opposite of impeccability. So, the epistemological model is not compatible with the notion of sin. The same goes in fact for the ontological model. If participation were possible, this might suggest that humans are capable of gradually overcoming their shortcomings. Yet the notion of sin completely destroys this model. In Augustine's view, there is only one possibility to overcome sin, and that is the grace bestowed by God on a sinner. There is not the slightest chance that the poor sinner might be able to defeat his own failures. If this were the case, God's existence would become contingent. His only reason to exist necessarily stems from the fact that no man can overcome his own faults. Were people be able to do so, God's existence would become contingent: He would only be needed in certain cases. Sin therefore, as conceived by Augustine, destroys the subtle argumentation the bishop himself used in both models, and it does not match either of these models. Why, then, did Augustine do this? Was he not aware of the contradictory nature of his argumentation? We will attempt to answer that question, but at this point the inevitable conclusion must be that the real reason for our moral confusion, our moral corruption, is still silenced.

Furthermore, it seems as though Augustine refuses to identify the sources of the moral swamp in which we live. The play in which we are all actors still has no script, and Augustine is not the one who is willing to write it. The only suggestion he offers is the story of the Fall and the original sin that resulted from it. However, we have already stated that this script is too little, too rude and too blunt.

Another approach to dissimilarity and of moral failure

Thus, Augustine leaves us with a sharply pictured problem, which apparently, he does not want to solve. Yet sometimes there are endeavours to find a kind of solution that does not appeal to the story of the Fall and original sin. When he discusses in *De ciuitate dei* the reasons why humans succumb to temptations, there is no direct reference to the Fall. Instead, Augustine draws on one of the two aforementioned models: namely the one based on participation and the notion of a layered reality. He wonders how it is possible that two people can both be equally impressed by the beauty of a body but make different choices. One will be seduced and move on to forbidden delights, whereas the other will not. What is the reason for this difference? It must be situated in our will. One of these two people will remain steadfast while the other will opt for some delights — both because they want to do so. One therefore will stick to the good will; the other chooses the evil one. How does this ill evil will produce itself? Where does it come from and is there any reason explaining the arrival of an ill will? The first step implies a turn to Neoplatonic concepts. It is the observation that a conundrum is caused by a form of wrong dynamic between *aversio* (turning away) and *conversio* (turning to; conversion). Normally speaking, the *aversio* should be understood as the result of being produced or generated by the divine unity – perhaps even a turning away from God. Conversion would then have to be interpreted as the return to this origin, the divine unity. This is a simple Neoplatonist scheme in which little can be found about irreparable errors. The dynamics between *aversio* and *conversio* have changed, though, in Augustine's mind. Angels have turned away from God and have not returned to Him. The cause of this absence of conversion is certainly a matter of pride. But where then did this pride come from? Augustine explains that an ill will produced this *aversio*. Next, then, from where does this ill will stem? For there should be at least a reason for this 'illness' of the will. Alas, Augustine's answer here is crystal clear: if someone were to ask for the *causa efficiens* of this ill will, he would find nothing: *nihil invenitur*![24] Now, if there is no *causa efficiens*, this only means that evil has no origin whatsoever and that it is impossible to identify its root. There is no root of evil because the root of all that exists is God, and therefore can only be good. It is impossible to suggest that He would be the origin of evil. So, if there is no origin of evil and no *causa efficiens* can be found, the only option left, according to Augustine, is a *causa deficiens*.[25] There simply is no reason – in the sense of *causa efficiens* – to explain why and how evil can suddenly become visible; there is simply no reason why the Fall happened; and there is no reason why among two people one will act morally impeccably whereas the other will behave like a monster. In the end, there is no answer to the question of evil. There is only the *causa deficiens*. This also eliminates the question of theodicy. It is obvious that God has nothing to do with evil, and if one were to raise the question as to why He nevertheless allows evil to happen, that would only compromise the Creator. The theodicy question suggests that God must have an answer regarding the existence of evil; however, that is incorrect. God does not owe us an answer to that question; every answer would immediately compromise his goodness. Moreover, the issue of *causa efficiens* and *causa deficiens* is more than wordplay. In Augustine's view, evil cannot be conceived of in the same way as the good. That would imply a relapse into Manichaeism, where the good and the evil

---

[24]*De Ciu.* XII,6: *Huius porro malae voluntatis causa efficiens si quaeratur nihil invenitur*. Some lines later: *nihil occurrit*. Cp also XII,9: *Cum ergo malae voluntatis efficiens naturalis vel, si dici potest, essentialis nulla sit causa*. See also and already *De Lib. Arb.* II,20,54: *Unde igitur erit? Ita quaerenti tibi, si respondeam nescire me*. Cp. William E. Mann, 'Augustine on Evil', in, David Vincent Meconi, ed., *The Cambridge Companion to Augustine*, Cambridge 2014, 58–107, who accepts Augustine's observation that there is no answer to the question of evil, but who does not analyse the element of the *causa deficiens*.

[25]*De Ciu.* XII,7: *Nemo igitur quaerat efficientem causam malae voluntatis; non enim est efficiens sed deficiens*.

are situated on an equal footing, which is unacceptable.[26] This is an understandable point of view; however, it remains somewhat unsatisfying. Basically, Augustine maintains the theory of Plotinus, who states that evil is the negation of something and which results in a complete deficiency. It is the negative connotation of something that exists *in se* and *per se*, for instance, unlimited compared to limit, non-measure compared to measure and so on.[27] This is the trail Augustine will follow, stating that evil is always the non-good compared to the Good, which results in the absence of the Good. This may be acceptable because it is understandable that Augustine will not frame the Good as the *causa efficiens* of evil: that would be an oxymoron. It does leave us, however, with the question of how to understand this absence, as an absence without any reason or explication. Now, an absence without any reason is difficult to understand. Normally speaking, the absence of something is caused by something else; for example, the absence of good health can be caused by illness, and the absence of freedom may be caused by a dictatorship, but a mere absence that has no cause is difficult to understand. It is the absence of the good and, in that sense, is related to the Good. Where, then, can we situate the relationship between the Good and the absence of it? If there is no reason, no explication, how then can we call it the absence of good? For if we call it the absence of good, this absence refers to something other than itself. It is no absence referring to absence; it is absence referring to the Good. Now, apparently, the solution of the *causa deficiens* is not a real solution because it does not explain why, on the one hand, we call it the absence of good whereas, on the other hand, we cannot explain why this absence still refers to the Good.

This is the reason that, in the end, the solution of the *causa deficiens* is not a satisfying one. Now if this is correct, can we then conclude, once again, that Augustine refuses to identify the problem he raised himself, the enigma of the dissimilarity? The answer will probably be affirmative. Yet there is a final possibility. In *De ciuitate dei* XIV, Augustine returns to the question he dealt

---

[26]Cp. Michel Sourisse, 'Saint Augustin et le problème du mal: la polémique antimanichéenne', *L'esprit du temps* 19(2007) 109–14.
[27]Cp. *Enn.* I,8. See, Dominic J. O'Meara, 'Explaining Evil in Late Antiquity', in Andrew P. Chignell ed, *Evil: A History*, Oxford 2019, 130–54.

with in book XII. This time, however, he does not mention the notion of a *causa deficiens*; no, there is another option he puts forward. In book XIV, he focuses on the difference between living according to oneself and living according to God. The first option is of course reprehensible, whereas the latter is to be followed. The bishop expands on this topic in many ways, but the core of his argument is the observation that *secundum se ipsum vivere* (to live according to oneself) is already a moment in which man turns away from God and that he, therefore, resembles the devil who also turned away from God.[28] In short, turning away from God is nothing less than sinning in its most obvious form. Augustine deals with this matter in depth and explains at length that man who is living according to himself cannot live according to God. It is living according to the flesh and, even more, it is living according to the lying nature of the devil. The true nature of man is to live according to Him by whom man has been created. That is his true nature, and if man does not live according to this true nature, he can only be considered to live in falsehood.[29] Should one, therefore, ask how to interpret the commandment to love one's neighbour as oneself, then the right explanation could only be that man has to love his neighbour as oneself according to God and not according to oneself.[30] In other words, there is no self independent of God. If one loves oneself, and this love is not according to God but according to one's self, then this love can only be a matter of cupidity.[31] This allows Augustine to conclude again that indeed there are two cities: one is the city in which self-love is the dominant character, and the other is the city in which the love of God prevails. When self-love precedes, it can only be qualified as the contempt of God, whereas the love of God brings about the contempt of oneself: *ad contemptum sui*.[32]

---

[28] *De Ciu.* XIV,4,1. An argumentation that is largely taken from earlier descriptions such as *De Gen. ad Litt.* XI,15,19; XI,26,33. Augustine finds the origin of the fall of the demon and all fallen angels in their pride (*superbia*). One might think that this superbia is rather comparable to the classical hybris.
[29] *De Ciu.* XIV,4,1.
[30] *De Ciu.* XIV, 7,1.
[31] *De Ciu.* XIV,7,2.
[32] *De Ciu.* XIV,28.

This is an important conclusion to keep in mind. Not only is there no human self outside God, but the right love of God can only produce a real contempt of one's own being. Let us be aware, moreover, that this contempt cannot be confused with a 'self-denying love', which has nothing to do with it – 'self-denying love' is mere condescension. Indeed, there is no righteous existence independent of God, and loving oneself according to God implies contempt of oneself.[33] Should one live according to one's nature, then such a life can only be a life that is similar to that of the devil, and which is in fact a lie (*mendacium*). The only permissible self-love is the love based on the firm conviction that man has been created by God, and all his love can therefore only regard this Creator. Once again, a human self-independent of God is inconceivable; it would suggest a man has his origin in himself, which is a suggestion that is nothing less than a lie. Contempt of oneself is, therefore, the justified result of loving God. It is in these words that one can discover the utter inner division with which Augustine was living. It is an ambiguity he did not manage to solve. Indeed, is it not awful to relate love and contempt so strongly together? Loving one implies despising the other, but this is the contradiction in its sharpest form. On the one hand, Augustine maintains – and never ceases to do so – that man is created according to the image of God. As we have seen, this can also imply that man is not only a being created according to the image of God, but that he is also an image of God. Certainly, he is so in a less splendid way than the Son, but being the image of God is man's glory nevertheless; he is connected to his Creator in a definite way. Even if he forgets this divine origin entirely, the heavenly image will remain present. The divine image cannot be lost. This is a positive appreciation of the essence of human existence, that there is a kind of divine spark in a human being that is so essential that it cannot be extinguished or lost. In other words, the image is the main motive

---

[33] I would disagree with David Meconi in his appreciation of self-loathing in Augustine. Self-loathing is not only an aspect of the perverted self, it is also a basic statement about the human condition. It is therefore astonishing that Meconi refers indeed to the myth of Narcissus and does so in a subtle way, but refuses to see that this myth leaves us with the enigma of love and contempt bound together. Cp. Fr. David Vincent Meconi, 'Ravishing Ruin: Self-Loathing in Saint Augustine', *Augustinian Studies* 45(2014) 227–46.

in a story that cannot be silenced or abolished. The image always refers to its original, which is the divine Creator. It is a play with a script and the image is the antagonist opposite to the protagonist. In that sense, it is a brilliant gift to human existence. There is a horizon that cannot be wiped out, contrary to the famous words of Nietzsche. This is the first impression in any case. Yet precisely in this text one encounters the opposite of this inspiring picture: the outline of a story dealing with failure, guilt and contempt. Man does indeed possess a divine image, but this image is more than he is worthy of. The divine image is a precious gift that has been spoiled; its message is that man ought to turn towards God, but it has been understood as a carte blanche to turn merely towards human existence. This is a great wrong that cannot be repaired – at least not by humans themselves. Or perhaps it should be formulated in another way. The divine image is also a commandment: it is not a sheer gift without any ulterior motive; it is a gift that represents a double agenda. Man must forget about his own nature, because there is no 'own' nature outside nature in the way God had defined it; there is no human nature as such. Contrary to plants and animals, who can be defined as *in se secundum suam similitudinem*[34] or as *secundum genus suum*,[35] man does not have an *in se* or a *genus suum*. Augustine avoids speaking about *secundum naturam* when he speaks about mankind, because there is no such thing as human nature. There is only the divine image which incorporates the real nature of man, which is none other than the turn towards God. The real commandment, therefore, is not to be human, but to be godlike. This implies contempt for one's own being. So, on the one hand, man's being is highly appreciated – gifted with the divine image – but on the other hand, this image is a commandment man can never fulfil. The image obliges him to forget about himself, to treat his own being with contempt and to accept that he must turn towards God while realizing he will never be able to do so. Augustine, putting it succinctly, depicts a beautiful image of a man and at the same time destroys it mercilessly. Indeed, he does so in a literally 'merciless' manner: without grace. The only element that might save a human being from this prison is God's grace. However, this grace is not

---

[34] Cp. *De Gen. contra Man.* I,13,19.
[35] *De Gen. Imp.* 11,34; 15,49; 16,54; *De Gen. ad Litt.* III,11,16 sqq.

something on which one can count. It must be an arbitrary gift, otherwise it no longer would be a gift, it would be a due.

The ultimate ambivalence: Love and contempt

In the end, the paradox we cannot solve is that contempt is part of love. This is the ultimate consequence of dissimilarity being part of similarity at an existential level. Augustine is a theologian capable of writing the most striking and beautiful pictures of humans, of humans longing for God, for love, for consolation; he is the one who has given us moving passages on what the relationship between God and man can be, but he has also crafted the most appalling pictures of the destruction of human dignity. What we find here is a highly ambiguous theory about the image of God, which is not only a gift but also a commandment. However, this latter aspect appears to be an unattainable goal. Hence, the original gift turns into doom and gloom. Once again, this is not only something to be considered regrettable because it leaves man with a self-destructive character from which he cannot escape; no, it also leaves unanswered the moral destruction we have so often witnessed. This means that Augustine does not expressly identify the cause of the inner destruction of man, but he does so implicitly, at an existential level. It is indeed by combining love and contempt that we discover the existential translation of dissimilarity integrated into similarity. Now it is contempt that is part of love and that cannot be put aside. Moreover, this contempt is not due to the Fall; no, it has to be there independently, whether we speak about *supra lapsum* or *infra lapsum*. However, this concept is an extremely dangerous one. It allows humans to pretend they care about others, that they even love them, but at the same time they can despise them. This is similar to saying 'You know, I even have Jews among my friends', or whichever group you want to mention on that slippery slope of love that becomes hate, but still pretends to be love. Here, at least, we can see how Augustine tried to love God but did so at the expense of His creatures. It is not God who sacrifices Himself; it is his creature who is expected to sacrifice himself. Alas, once this connection has become a cultural expression of the dynamics of

Christian belief, the contempt will have no boundaries anymore and will always hit those we consider inferior, although at the same time we pretend to love them. There will no longer be any need to refer to colonialism and its modern versions such as racism, anti-Semitism, sexual abuse and so on. If, then, we ask ourselves how this double Augustinian image can be related to the modern structures of the concept of the image, we can still clearly distinguish the two sides. There is an attractive side, of an image that has fully retained its referential power and which still reveals a greater reality than it can express itself, but there is also the image that refuses to refer to anything whatsoever, because the 'commandment' to truly refer to a wider and deeper world than the one it shows itself cannot be realized. This image is doomed to fail, so there is no reason why it should continue to pretend to refer to something else. It is self-sufficient and considers this self-sufficiency the only possibility in a world that, while lacking a story about values, cannot return to the old story in which God is accusing man of not being capable of fulfilling his commandments, knowing it to be impossible. The image then becomes self-referential and, therefore, it is a script without a play. Love and contempt as a double commandment is perhaps what our modern image represents most. We love our images, but we also hate them. They constantly need to be improved, but this constantly proves to be impossible. The message that is passed on is a catastrophic one; if our love is steeped in contempt, there is very little chance that we will not end up as split beings, who can pretend they love some people but that do not feel guilty about contemning others. This, then, is perhaps one of the roots of moral destruction.[36] That is the fearful conclusion we have to draw. Yet there is no reason to consider Augustine as the beginning of an anti-humanist tradition. We must insist on the fact that he wanted to put forward a double point of view, although neither approach matches the other. But, as he did so, we must also look at the ways he tried to preserve the referential character of the image. He was of course aware of the possibility that, by insisting too much on the dissimilarity, there would be no reference left at all. Was there still any possibility of approaching the similarity without denying

---

[36] Cp. Joseph Haward, *The Ghost of Perfection: Searching for Humanity*, Eugene Oregon 2017.

dissimilarity, without making the latter the ultimate parameter in the whole relationship between God and man? He at least tried to do so through analysing the role of our memory. Memory: this strange country, belonging to past and present, where God and humans might meet.

A second ambivalence: Who is who in our memory?

Augustine was fascinated by memory and he worked on this theme many times. It is a human capacity that is easily accessible. Everyone can easily recall things from the past and we constantly use our memory and memories: you remember where you put your keys yesterday; you recall the rain that was falling a week ago; you remember the joy of having a holiday. So, indeed, we constantly use our memory and memories, but we do not realize how complex memory is. This is what intrigues Augustine and is what he tries to understand in book X of *Confessions*. Could we deem it possible that God is also part of our memory? Or, to put it more precisely, that He dwells in our memory? If so, where then can we find God in our memory and, if memory is a human capacity, is it correct to argue that God is within the reach of our memory? Is memory indeed the level playing-field between God and man? Augustine dealt with all these questions and seriously tried to not outrun them. Yet they are complicated, and they become even more complicated once one tries to establish the relationship between memory and image. How, then, did Augustine proceed?

He starts in book X, in fact, with a general overview of what exactly memory is. He does so in order to look for a relationship between God and memory. Yet, before so doing, he had already undertaken a quest for God by looking at creation. Indeed, creation is wonderful and it can rightly be admired, but the whole creation had only taught him that, notwithstanding its beauty, it certainly was not God.[37] On the contrary: it was created by Him. The main argument Augustine used to put forward this point of view was,

---

[37] *Conf.* X,6.8.

of course, an anti-Manichaean one: all these visible parts of the creation had body-like structures and hence they could not be God; God is not this earth or heaven, nor is He any kind of body. Is it not true that a body cannot be vivified by another body? It can only be given life by a soul. Indeed, there is something that transcends the bodily structures of this life, and that is our soul. The soul, then, gives life to us and, in the same way, it is God who is the life of our lives.[38] Having learned this and having made short work of the Manichaeans, Augustine now turns to his memory and continues his quest for God. It is a search that will lead him in different directions but the description he presents of this quest belongs to the most attractive chapters of *Confessions*. Memory, he argues in a most vivid and colourful picture, has a double nature. On the one hand, memory can be compared to a great hall where all kind of memories are stored. It is an extremely attractive treasury, which is particularly due to the immense variety of memories that have been stored here. This variety does not have a kind of passive quality, as if memories were golden coins lying immovable, heaped up against the walls of this vast building. No, memories are rather like animals: some of them shy, hiding, others gay, jumping to the one who looks for them. That is the first image of our memory as it figures in X,8,12: of memory as a huge building where all our memories are stocked, independently of their nature. The second image then, in X,17,26, is that of our memory as some sort of large field one strolls around looking at the many caves found in this landscape. Again, the landscape has no boundaries; one cannot see any horizon indicating the end of this incredible countryside. Both images, therefore, depict our memory as something where all the memories are stored: a palace with many rooms or a wide landscape, each storing different memories. In that sense, memory is not so much a warehouse or landscape, but rather an infinity. The palace where all our memories are stocked knows of no walls, it is rather a room with a door that opens to another room, with a door opening to another room, and so on.

---

[38]*Conf.* X,6,10: 'Non est deus tuus terra et caelum neque omne corpus'. Hoc dicit eorum natura. Vident: moles est, minor in parte quam in toto. Iam tu melior es, tibi dico, anima, quoniam tu vegetas molem corporis tui praebens ei vitam, quod nullum corpus praestat corpori. Deus autem tuus etiam tibi vitae vita est.

But memory is not only a huge room, it is not only a landscape where one can find memories lying under a tree or hiding in a cave no, memory is also an activity in itself. It is the activity of storing in different rooms or different drawers, depending on the nature of each memory. Memory, therefore, is not a passive room, just a storehouse; it is also the activity of thinking, and that is the reason Augustine considers it part of our mind. As such, it is responsible for combining memories, of awakening almost sleeping memories and bringing them together. Memory, in its active form, is comparable to, for example, the capacity of picking up food from the stomach – [39] as the bishop of Hippo explains in a rather explicit metaphor. We can remember our main feelings – desire, joy, sadness and fear – without experiencing them again; I can now recall my fear without being anxious; I can speak about sadness without grieving. All of this demonstrates that memory has an active quality. It is not only a storehouse; it actively stores and works hard to create a kind of order inside this huge palace. That is why there exists, in Augustine's view, a correspondence between bringing together and thinking, between the Latin verbs *cogere* and *cogitare*, as he puts it in X,11,18. This being said, this element only emphasizes the infinity that belongs to memory. Not only is the number of memories infinite, but also the activity of thinking and ranging all these memories is an activity without boundaries.

Indeed, it is an activity, but this activity is difficult to understand. Of course a memory can be stored somewhere, but there are many contradictory aspects that remain difficult to resolve. One can forget something, for instance, and at the same time remember that one has forgotten. How is it possible to remember what one has forgotten? If this oblivion were something powerful, it would have enhanced its own force, and what has been forgotten would really have been forgotten. On the other hand, if oblivion is present in our memory, is it then present *in* our memory or does it exist *next* to our memory? Or to quote another example: if I speak of my memory, I can only do so by recalling it – I remember in fact that I remember. Yet, if this is the case, is this first memory then present in our memory or is it only an image? If it is an image of our memory, it cannot be inside memory itself; hence should we conclude that our

---

[39] *Conf.* X,14,22.

memory is only present as itself thanks to an image? As Augustine puts it: *Num et ipsa per imaginem suam sibi adest ac non per se ipsam?*[40] The question is justified, but at least it also shows that our mind is aware of itself. The question is not only a question: it is also proof. This whole picture is required to raise the question whether God can in fact be found in our memory. Memory, apparently, is so vast and huge that one hardly knows where to look for God. Not only is it vast and huge, but in its active form it is also stuffed with contradictions, which are far from easy to resolve. Nevertheless, God must be found in man's memory. Otherwise, if man were to find God outside his memory, he would not be able to remember God. How then could he find Him if he did not remember Him?[41] Now, in order to avoid a circular argument, Augustine changes his perspective and argues that everyone is interested in being happy. This is one of the rare questions that everyone would answer in the same way; not everyone opts for the same profession, but everyone would answer affirmatively when asked whether one wanted to be happy. The next step is to argue that everyone loves the truth, and that happiness is nothing other than sticking to the truth. This is, of course, a conclusion drawn somewhat too easily – a form of jumping to conclusions – but Augustine talks his way out by arguing that no one loves to be deceived and therefore that everyone loves the truth.[42] Having reached this stage, he can now draw his final conclusion: he has looked for God in every corner of his memory, but still he looked for a place, for a room in this wonderful palace called memory, where the lord of the castle is the castle itself. Nonetheless, looking for a place comes down to forgetting that truth does not dwell in any place. Once one remembers the truth, one finds God in his memory. After that miraculous conclusion, Augustine proceeds with some of the most moving lines of the *Confessions*, the *sero te amavi*.[43] So the conclusion can be clear: God does not 'dwell' in any physical sense of the word, but he can be found in our memory. There must therefore be a connection between memory and God,

---

[40]*Conf.* X,15,23.
[41]*Conf.* X,17,26.
[42]*Conf.* X,23,33.
[43]*Conf.* X,27,38. Late I came to love Thee. A comparison of different translations can be found at: https://epistleofdude.wordpress.com/2019/05/14/a-comparison-of-different-translations-of-augustines-confessions-late-have-i-loved-you/.

but this connection cannot be a very simple one. If we look at the main characteristics of our memory – storehouse, activity of the mind, as well as lord of the castle – then it will be clear that God has no place in the storehouse. He does not belong to our memories in the same way as our other memories. In speaking of our memory as an activity of our mind, it is also clear that God does not belong to our mental activities; He is not our mind. Instead, He is the Lord God of our mind: *nec ipse animus es, quia Dominus Deus animi tu es.*[44] So, even if He could be part of the mental activities, He cannot be identified with them. Finally, to be perfectly clear, Augustine repeats for the last time that God cannot be compared to any image of physical objects. Certainly not, although the reader of his *Confessions* will probably consider this as a kind of redundancy, but it raises the question of the image in a new way. God does not dwell in our memory as in a kind of concrete house or palace. He is therefore not comparable to any memory that we can say that is literally stored in this palace. Memories that can be stored often do have a physical aspect, yet, although He does not dwell in our memory, God can be found in it. Hence, the only possible way out is to assume that our memory must have the quality of an image, a non-physical image, of God. How can we define this image? That is the problem Augustine approaches in *De Trinitate*. There, he focuses not so much on memory as the 'place' where God can be found, as on memory as the active capacity of man to remember and to find God. This implies that memory is surely not only an analogy but that it also functions as an anagogical approach. Would it have been merely an ontological definition, it could have excluded an analogical approach. However, now that Augustine focuses mainly on memory as an active element, it has to be considered as an anagogical means.[45] However, Augustine's augmentation is highly complicated and scholars have long debated on the correct meaning

---

[44] *Conf.* X,25,36.
[45] Cp. R. J. Teske, 'The Image and Likeness of God in St. Augustine's *De Genesi* ad *Litteram Liber Imperfectus*', *Augustinianum* 30(1990) 441–51, where the author discusses the opinion of O. du Roy who considers the *ad* in *ad imaginem dei* as an anagogical approach. The point is highly important one and our enquiry on the very nature of the image has to take into account this difference.

of his picture.[46] Indeed, the way Augustine deals with memory and image is far from easy, and sometimes downright complex, as if the author himself had his doubts about where to go and how to attain his goal.

All in all, although memory has many aspects and although Augustine tries to define them as clearly as possible, he does so in order to see how similarity and dissimilarity can be transferred to other fields, and to choose another approach from this terminological and ontological couple. Memory, in this sense, is an ideal field in which to conduct research: it concerns the past and the present and covers both similarity as well as dissimilarity. What becomes visible is that Augustine seems to opt for an approach that favours similarity. Admittedly, God does not dwell in our memory in any literal sense of the words, but memory seems to be the only road giving access to the divine presence.

---

[46] Cheuk Yin Yam and Anthony Dupont, 'A Mind-Centered Approach of "Imago Dei": A Dynamic Construction in Augustine's De Trinitate XV', *Augustiniana* 62(2012) 7–43 try to re-establish a balance between an ontological and epistemological approach of the '*imago Dei*', favouring the epistemological approach. The article is a welcome correction of scholarly reception. However, it starts with the idea of *imago Dei* as a biblical notion whereas Augustine is clearly not arguing in a biblical way when he deals in detail with the *imago Dei* as I have tried to make clear.

5

De Trinitate

How did Augustine continue his quest in *De Trinitate*? If memory is an active capacity of man, and if it partly defines the notion of image, how then does he proceed with this complex matter? To begin, Augustine establishes a relationship between image and memory by insisting on the role both elements play in the domain of knowledge. For knowledge, according to Augustine, is not something neutral, something comparable to an object that suddenly presents itself to our eyes and mind thanks to some manoeuvres of the mind. Let us say, for example, that thanks to a process of abstraction, we can categorize what we see and then define it according to previously prepared parameters. No; knowledge is a kind of process in which many actors play their role. There is, of course, the subject, but there is also something that may be called the object, but which is sometimes more than a mere 'object'. There is our memory, there are images, there is the need to rectify our impressions, there is the desire to know and so on; all these aspects have their role to play, but the script is not always clear. Yes, the goal is knowledge, but knowledge of a table, for example, differs widely from the knowledge of love of God. Consequently, all the elements mentioned have different roles, depending on the knowledge that is strived for. For instance, desire can be important when it comes to love but it can be less important when our attention is drawn to the table. So the script of this play is partly unpredictable yet, at the same time, large structures will remain the same. If, for instance, desire plays either a more or a less important role, this does not change the fact that it always focuses on knowledge. Now, in this play, Augustine focuses on knowledge of God, and in this particular script the well-known elements such as love, desire, memory and image will again occupy the scene. We will not expand too much on love and desire; instead, we need to focus on memory and image. Both are notions that easily overlap, although they are far from identical. Many memories have nothing to do with image and many images cannot be identified with memories at all. Nevertheless, they often overlap and the way Augustine analyses these intersecting roads is fascinating.

Some general remarks on *De Trinitate*

For the sake of argument, our enquiry starts in book VIII of *De Trinitate*, where Augustine sets out the different options for obtaining knowledge of God. It is a quest conducted in a subtle manner, although perhaps somewhat enigmatically. Augustine does not apply a clear method; instead he proceeds in an almost intuitive way. Nonetheless, there is a clear starting point. Now that the author has reflected on the Trinity as it can be laid out by the Scriptures in the first four books, and now that he has tried to discuss the philosophical aspects of this doctrine in books V–VII, he turns to the mystery of the Trinity in a more mystical way, so to speak. Of course, the second part of *De Trinitate* (books VIII–XV) has always been seen as the 'psychological' part of the work, but I doubt this. It is the unfolding of the idea that the Trinity is not only a belief, a conviction we have to understand, but also the bewildering awareness that we are able, at least partly, to understand its mystery. There is a desire to understand the Trinity that, to some extent, can be fulfilled. It is this desire, this awareness of our understanding, that obliges us to turn to this desire itself and wonder whether the Trinity itself is not the heart of this desiring dynamic. This second part is therefore, in my view, not the description of how one can try to understand the Trinity; it is the unfolding of a thesis that one cannot desire in such an ardent way without being touched by Desire itself in the most intimate way. This Desire is nothing less than the Trinity. It is a concept that seems to be inspired by *Enneads* V, meaning that if the Trinity itself is the heart of our longing for the Trinity, then it must be present in our longing in some way. Trinity and desire are almost intersecting, implying that to look for the Trinity is nothing other than the Trinity itself longing for its own unfolding into a fascinating diversity. It is the divine 'I' longing to unfold itself into a 'Me', comparable the loving subject, the One, longing for the beloved One. There is, in other words, a form of self-reference that is longing for differentiation, and it is this aspect of self-reference that we will come across in the paragraphs below. I will attempt to explain this in more detail, but such an approach is quite different from current ideas that suggest we have an original, the Trinity, that can be recognized in certain patterns humans have in themselves. In that case, the relationship between God and man would be that of a kind of allegory, and the one who understands the Trinity only needs to see these parallels in order to grasp the Trinity. Admittedly, that would be a process that still is far from easy to accomplish, but essentially it would be nothing other than abstracting, transcending or extrapolating. That is indeed the often – practised way of interpreting this second part of *De Trinitate*. It is a process similar to arguing that there must be a wonderful cube in a dimension we can hardly grasp. Fortunately, we know that in our present reality there are cubes; as such, we can make a reliable sketch of this wonderful cube in another dimension by basing ourselves on the properties of ordinary cubes, and then concluding that this wonderful cube must be similar to the ordinary one but simultaneously dissimilar. The wonderful cube cannot be physical; it should resemble the mathematical one, but it would still linger in the mathematical world as a comparison, incapable of grasping the cube's reality itself. So, the current model and its way of connecting the ordinary cubes to the wonderful one implies that there is still an intellect surveying both cubes and even drawing conclusions on the most particular cube that exists. In reality, however, there is no such thing as an external intellect surveying both cubes. No, there is a mind discovering its own cube-like form, thanks to the fact that it is a cube. The cube discovers that it is a cube, not thanks to other cubes with which it can be compared, but thanks to the mere fact of being a cube itself. Admittedly this is a strange phenomenon: this self-discovery due to one's own structure. However, it is a crucial step that Augustine takes here and one he applies at different moments. It is a motive present in many of his arguments, such as when he explains how the mind discovers itself as a thinking reality, the famous Augustinian *cogito* in *De Trinitate*. X,10,14, or when he speaks about love that discovers its own structure in *De Trinitate*. IX,2,2. He constantly refers to realities that also create their own reality – difficult though this may be to understand. That is why we so often come across arguments such as 'One cannot love what one has not known previously'. Or 'One can only know God if God bestows him this knowledge'. All these arguments tend to demonstrate the highly complex relationship between reflection and reality. Therefore, Augustine mainly attempts to relate thinking and being in a way that counters their normal relationship, according to which thinking is a reflection of and on reality. Indeed, they are normally separated, and thinking is an endeavour to understand reality – a reality that is separated from reflection and that continues to exist once one stops thinking about it. Think, for instance, of a tree. When I see a tree, I consider it to have a certain substance, that it is an object that is planted somewhere, that it is related to the ground on which it stands, and that it has a certain age. Thinking about the tree is to try to understand a small part of our reality. However, the tree and the reflection on this tree remain separated. The tree will still be there once I no longer think of it. Yet, my ideas on a particular tree are far from evident. I will compare it to other trees I have seen, and I will notice some similarities as well as some dissimilarities. Hence, what I have concluded on this particular tree by thinking of it is already difficult to generalize. In all of these cases, however, thinking remains a tool I use and which I try to apply to reality – a tool that can be useful but that by definition cannot be identical to reality. The tree I am thinking of is not the real one. The real one is somewhere in, let us say, a forest or a garden, and I only have a kind of reproduction in my head.

Now, what really differs in Augustine's doctrine of the Trinity from these accounts of ordinary objects is that he does not consider our mind as a lesser reproduction or reflection of the Trinity, allowing us to understand the real Trinity by abstracting from the lesser conditions in which human trinitarian structures exist. No, what Augustine aims for is to show that the reality of the Trinity creates a new reality, similar though different, identical though not equal, making it possible to understand the divine Trinity. Therefore, even the word 'understanding' can easily be misunderstood. The Augustinian vocabulary uses in these cases the word *intellectus*, which etymologically means 'reading between', namely between thinking and being. It is a notion including in this particular case the divine and the human reality, and it expresses that these two are different and yet similar, or even identical. *Intellectus* shows that

there is only a single reality that cannot be interpreted as having
different layers, as in the Platonic tradition, but one that creates its
understanding. Indeed, that is what Augustine sees as the essence
of this doctrine: we are talking about the Trinity creating its own
understanding, its own *intellectus*. This is not by having a mirror in
front of it, called the human mind, but by a differentiation in which
the one single reality becomes a twofold structure. It refers to itself
and at the same time it refers to another. On the one hand, there is
being and reflection, which may be called Father and Son; on the
other hand, there is God and man. That is the basis of the approach,
and it is a wonderful one. Evidently, however, one runs into many
difficulties by focusing on such an approach. How, for instance,
can such an approach be matched with the model of a Creator and
creation, characterized by a sharp divide between both terms? Or,
to touch on another difficulty, how can the relationship between
Father and Son become comparable to the one that exists between
God and man? How can we match divine immanence and economy,
how can we harmonize such an otology with soteriology? The most
important problem, however, that threatens the magnificence of
the Trinity creating its own understanding, is perhaps the following
one, which opposes ontology and soteriology. There is this
'understanding' of the Father, which can rightly be called the Son
because it is the product of the unique and simple One. However, as
soon as this Son, seen from a soteriological point of view, becomes
associated with 'grace', the whole system risks falling apart. Grace
is only bestowed on a minority of people, whereas the idea of an
unfolding Trinity cannot be applied to a small minority. Christology
and Trinity in that case may become contradicting theologies. That is
the obvious danger of insisting too much on the role of Christology
as the gateway to soteriology within the trinitarian theology.[1] Of
course, seen from an immanent point of view, the Son continues
to be the second form of a unique reality that will always last
because there is no Trinity conceivable that has not created its own
intellectus. Within the framework of the economy, however, it risks
turning the whole system upside down. That is one of the major
tensions within the Augustinian doctrine of the Trinity: soteriology

---

[1] Cp. Lewis Ayres, 'The Christological Context of Augustine's *De Trinitate XIII*: Towards Relocating Books VIII–XV', *Augustinian Studies* 29(1998) 111–39.

tearing apart and spoiling the integrity of the trinitarian ontology. This is something that was foreshadowed in *Confessions*, where Augustine insisted on the fact that the Platonists understood the divine truth but that, unfortunately, the name of Christ was lacking.[2] All this is based on the idea of the absolute divide, of the unbridgeable gap between the human and the divine, which gives birth to the idea that the human part of this divide can only function as a kind of 'analogy' – a popular notion in the scholarly comments on *De Trinitate*. In my view, however, Augustine's epistemology does not apply the ordinary division between reflection and being that would justify the use of the term 'analogy', which in the end remains a notion suggesting such a divide.[3] Indeed, analogy is a term that has already absorbed the distance between ontology and soteriology, so to speak, and that can be seen as an effort to connect these two approaches to each other, and thus 'solve' the problem of a scattered unity. In a more restricted way, 'analogy' is a term that is even compatible with the idea of a divine grace bestowed to only a small minority, an arbitrary gift that will allow a few people to bridge the gap between the divine and the human. Whereas in fact, Augustine has tried to show how, within the Trinity, a new reality has been created inside an already existing reality. It is for this reason that I do not consider the term 'analogy' a useful one, although its attractiveness is understandable. The term serves to reduce the impact of Augustine's miraculous efforts to discover new ways instead of maintaining a binary system of separated entities. Later we will return to this tension in Augustine's trinitarian theology, which gives birth to models of analogy. What matters now is to see how this idea of a reality creating a new reality can be applied to the notions of image and memory. Augustine tries to do so in a most admirable way.

---

[2] Cp. *Conf.* VII,9,13–15. I do not agree with Luigi Gioia, who states in his *The Theological Epistemology of Augustine's De Trinitate*, Oxford 2008 (ch 4) that Augustine's epistemology has to be seen as part of his soteriology or as subdued to his soteriology. There is constant tension between these two aspects and looking at the role of the image in both soteriology and epistemology, it seems to me one cannot reduce epistemology to soteriology.

[3] Cp. Lewis Ayres, '"Remember That You Are Catholic" (serm. 52.2): Augustine on the Unity of the Triune God', *Journal of Early Christian Studies* 8(2000) 39–82, who constantly speaks of analogies.

However, now that we have anticipated future trains of thought somewhat, this is certainly the moment we need to discuss the vast literature on Augustine, and in particular his doctrine of the Trinity. It is useless to picture a real *status quaestionis* of the scholarly research on *De Trinitate*, which has been done in a marvellous way by Kany.[4] What perhaps is more important is to observe some general tendencies, which I would consider to be a kind of 'Christianization' of Augustine. On the one hand, this is a great discovery from the past few years: Christology not as a doctrine but as an inner voice that constantly returns and returns, trying to catch its fascination for a Voice that evokes all other voices, as was masterfully shown by Miles Hollingworth.[5] It is about Augustine as an author, as a brilliant writer who easily manages to enchant his readers, leaving them with the question of how he succeeded in doing so. On the other hand, there is also a form of return to Augustinian Christology as the essence not only of his doctrine (if ever there was such a thing) but of Christianity itself. There has been ongoing debate on the authors and ideas that influenced Augustine, and barely any of the then contemporary schools and religious movements have been left aside when it comes to having influenced the bishop of Hippo. Of course, he himself mentions Platonism, Neoplatonism, Plotinus and Porphyry, but also the Sceptics and the Stoics. As a matter of fact, once one starts to read books VII, XIV and XIX of *De ciuitate dei*, one recognizes that Augustine tries to engage in the debates of his time. This is something he does from the very beginning of his writings, reflecting on the theme of 'if Plato had lived (now)'[6] and concluding that you only need to 'change some tiny words'[7] to see that Platonism and Christianity are quite similar. Next to this 'philosophical' debate there is a Christian heritage: first of all, the Bible, but perhaps even more

---

[4]Roland Kany, *Augustins Trinitätsdenken*, Tübingen 2007.
[5]Miles Hollingworth, 'Closer to Augustine: Speculating on the Recent Past, and Future, of Augustine Scholarship', *The Expository Times* 125 (2013) 220–9. Professor van Bavel had already in his time showed the extreme relevance of the Christology, see, Tarcisius J. Van Bavel, *Recherches sur la christologie de saint Augustin. L'humain et le divin dans le Christ d'après saint Augustin*, Fribourg 1954.
[6]*De Vera Rel.* 3,3.
[7]*De Vera Rel.* 4,7.

the theological tradition we can find in Ambrose, Marius Victorinus, Jerome, Tertullian, Cyprian and so on. The picture is a complicated one and anyone familiar with the scholarly research on Augustine, in particular his work on the Trinity, knows how the frontline goes back and forth. There is no need to recall the 'the old ghost of Lord Alfaric',[8] but the influence of (Neo-)Platonism is undisputed and it contradicts the oft-used model of the Augustinian doctrine of analogies within the Trinity.[9] Research by scholars such Luc Brisson,[10] John Turner,[11] Philip Carey,[12] John Rist,[13] R. A. Markus,[14] Mark Edwards[15] and in an earlier phase A. H. Armstrong[16] and Pierre Hadot,[17] has discovered how broad the field of Platonism was in these early days of the current era, and that it cannot be clearly separated, or even distinguished, from the currents which we later have come to call 'Christian'. The same goes for the terms 'Christian' and 'philosophical'; there is a tendency to emphasize a particular antagonism between these traditions, which causes

---

[8] Ian Clausen, *On Love, Confession, Surrender and the Moral Self*, New York 2018, 44. Prosper Alfaric, *L'évolution intellectuelle de saint Augustin*, Paris 1918.
[9] The tradition that started with M. Schmaus, *Die psychlogische Trinitätslehre des heligen Augustinus*, Münster 1927.
[10] Luc Brisson, 'The Reception of the Parmenides before Proclus', *Zeitschrift für Antikes Christentum* 12(2008) 99–113, Idem, 'Reminiscence in Plato', in John Dillon, Marie-Elise Zovko, eds., *Platonism and Forms of Intelligence*, Berlin 2008, 179–90.
[11] John Turner, ed., *Plato's Parmenides and Its Heritage. Volume 1: History and Interpretation from the Old Academy to Later Platonism and Gnosticism*, Leiden/Boston 2010; Volume II, *Reception in Patristic, Gnostic and Christian Neoplatonic Texts*, Leiden/Boston 2010.
[12] Philip Carey, *Augustine's Invention of the Inner Self: The Legacy of a Christian Platonist*, Oxford 2003; Idem, *Outward Signs: The Powerlessness of External Things in Augustine's Thought*, Oxford/New York 2008.
[13] John M. Rist, *Augustine: Ancient Thought Baptised*, Cambridge 1994.
[14] R. A. Markus, *Christianity and the Secular*, Notre Dame Press 2006; Idem, *Saeculum: History and Society in the Theology of St. Augustine*, Cambridge 1970/89.
[15] Mark Edwards, *Catholicity and Heresy in the Early Church*, London 2009; Idem, *Image, Word and God in the Early Christian Centuries*, London 2013.
[16] A. H. Armstrong, *Saint Augustine and Christian Platonism*, Villanova 1967; Idem (with R. A. Markus), *Christian Faith and Greek Philosophy*, Sheed 1964.
[17] Pierre Hadot, *Porphyre et Victorinus*, Paris 1968. Idem, *Etudes de Philosophie Ancienne*, Paris 1998.

their similarities to be overlooked.[18] That research partly overlaps with the research of Judith Lieu,[19] who demonstrated that the notion of 'Christian' as the denominator of a clear identity was a fluid one, and that it would be extremely difficult to reveal the particular characteristics of these Christian communities as compared to other religious communities. It was only afterwards that 'heretics' such as Marcion were made, as she shows. Comparable research has been conducted by Markus Vinzent[20] on the early history of Christianity, whereas Christoph Markschies has pictured Christianity as one of the possibilities on the religious market.[21] All these scholars have insisted on the fact that Late Antiquity brought forth its own continuation and that there was not suddenly a new movement turning a whole culture upside down. On the other hand, scholars such as Lewis Ayres,[22] in particular, have shown in a subtle and detailed way how the Trinitarian doctrine was based on earlier forms of orthodoxy. It is research that insists on a Christian tradition that gradually came into existence, indeed with many Neoplatonist influences, but which was yet quite different from the various philosophical and religious currents that can be identified in Late Antiquity.[23] This research can be

---

[18] The finest description of these approaches is to be found in Robert Crouse, 'Paucis mutatis verbis: St Augustine's Platonism', in Robert Dodaro, George Lawless, eds., *Augustine and His Critics*, New York 2000, 37–50. It is amazing to read first the contribution of Crousse and then, in the next chapter, the vision of Lewis Ayres: 'The Fundamental Grammar of Augustine's Trinitarian Theology', *ibid*, 51–76. We almost look at two different worlds.

[19] Judith Lieu, *Marcion and the Making of a Heretic: God and Scripture in the Second Century*, New York 2014; Idem, *Christian Identity in the Jewish and Graeco-Roman World*, Oxford 2004.

[20] Markus Vinzent, *Writing the History of Early Christianity: From Reception to Retrospection*, Cambridge 2019.

[21] Christoph Markschies, *Gnosis und Christentum*, Berlin 2009.

[22] Lewis Ayres, *Augustine and the Trinity*, Cambridge 2010. Idem, *Nicaea and Its Legacy. An Approach to Fourth-Century Trinitarian Theology*, Oxford 2004. Ayres starts his book with a chapter on Olivier du Roy, the scholar who, in my view, wrote a brilliant book on the neoplatonic character of Augustine early trinitarian theologies. Cp. Olivier du Roy, *L'intelligence de la foi en la Trinité selon saint Augustin*, Paris 1966.

[23] Cp also the beautiful book of Gerald Bonner, *Freedom and Necessity: St Augustine's Teaching on Divine Power and Human Freedom*, Washington 2007.

seen as the intensification of the work of scholars in the 1980s and 1990s, such as Goulven Madec,[24] who could not agree with the brilliant study of Olivier du Roy. I admire and hold in high esteem the work of such scholars as Frances Young,[25] Gerald Bonner,[26] Lewis Ayres, Rowan Williams,[27] Carol Harrison,[28] Robert Dodaro,[29] Johannes Brachtendorf[30] and Isabelle Bochet,[31] to name just a few, but I find it hard to avoid the impression of Christianization in a doctrinal sense of Augustine.[32] This is something we have also seen in the contributions of Radical Orthodoxy[33] and Charles Taylor.[34] Of course, Augustine was a Christian and, of course, he experienced a conversion (at least so we think), but the whole of his reflection is embedded in the structures and dynamics of Late Antiquity and I cannot see how we can escape essentialism and anachronism if we do not admit that early Christianity has very little to do with our reception of these times. In this respect, it is a pity that relatively little has

---

[24] G. Madec, 'Notes sur l'intelligence augustinienne de la foi', *REAug* 17(1971) 119–42.

[25] Frances Young, 'Augustine's Hermeneutics and Postmodern Criticism', *A Journal of Bible and Theology* 58(2004) 42–55; Idem, *Biblical Exegesis and the Formation of Christian Culture*, Cambridge 1997.

[26] Gerald Bonner, *Freedom and Necessity: St. Augustine's Teaching on Divine Power and Human Freedom*, Washington 2007.

[27] Rowan Williams, *On Augustine*, London, New York 2016.

[28] Carol Harrison, *Augustine: Christian Truth and Fractured Humanity*, Oxford 2000. Idem, *Rethinking Augustine's Early Theology. An Argument for Continuity*, Oxford 2006.

[29] Robert Dodaro, George Lawless, eds., *Augustine and His Critics: Essays in Honour of Gerald Bonner*, London/New York 2000.

[30] Johannes Brachtendorf, *Die Struktur des Menslichen Geistes nach Augustinus. Selbstreflexion und Erkenntnis Gottes in De Trinitate*, Tübingen 1998. Idem (ed.), *Gott und Sein Bild – Augustinus' De Trinitate im Spiegel gegenwärtiger Forschung*, Paderborn 2000.

[31] Isabelle Bochet, *Saint Augustin et le désir de Dieu*, Paris 1982.

[32] Another example, Marie-Anne Vannier, *Saint Augustin*, Paris 2011. See also Michel René Barnes, 'Rereading Augustine's Theology of the Trinity', in Stephen T. Davis, Daniel Kendall and Gerald O'Collins, eds., *The Trinity: An Interdisciplinary Symposium on the Trinity*, Oxford, 2001, 145–76.

[33] For instance, Michael Hanby, *Augustine and Modernity*, London 2003.

[34] Charles Taylor, *Sources of the Self: The Making of Modern Identity*, Harvard 1989.

been published on the relationship between Augustinian theology and our modern culture. There are some exceptions – sometimes very inspiring exceptions – such as the St Augustine Lecture of John Rist,[35] the fascinating work of Miles Hollingworth on Augustine and Wittgenstein,[36] the works of R. A. Markus[37] and scholars such as Markus Vinzent; perhaps also, in a certain way, those of Radical Orthodoxy. However, what is lacking is the awareness that our moral universe has largely been shaped by Christianity and that Christianity in its modern outlook still bears many features derived from Augustinian theology. The original debate between Julian of Aeclanum and Augustine was not about perfectionism or rigorism, nor about the role or preeminence of grace, but about the possibility to live according to certain moral standards that can never be put aside. Julian claimed that morality cannot be lost because it is a divine gift that never fades away; Augustine rejected this position because it might compromise God's ultimate freedom to bestow grace or not. But his thesis left unanswered the question of how to construct morality once it can no longer be founded in human nature or, more importantly once it cannot be founded in God anymore. The latter possibility must be put aside once one realizes that, in Augustine's doctrine, God's decisions have become entirely contingent. This is a contingency emphasized by the fact that, whatever God does, it is good because He does it; there is no longer a platonic Good allowing the Demiurge to be inspired by this Good. These aspects over-emphasize the contingency of what is good and why it is good. The question of the possibility of any morality and of the Augustinian heritage in this matter is rarely dealt with in

---

[35] John M. Rist, 'Democracy and Religious Values. Augustine on Locke, Lying and Individualism', St. Augustine Lecture 1997, *Augustinian Studies* 29(1998) 7–24. Rist was to repeat in detail his vision of Augustine and the harmful reception of his thoughts in later times in his *Augustine Deformed*, Cambridge 2014.
[36] Miles Hollingworth, *Saint Augustine of Hippo: An Intellectual Biography*, Oxford 2013; Idem, *Ludwig Wittgenstein*, Oxford 2018.
[37] R. A. Markus, *Saeculum: History and Society in the Theology of St. Augustine*, Cambridge 1970.

secondary literature.[38] The Platonic heritage of this debate on the possibility of morality, ranging from the *Gorgias* to the *Republic*, seems to be forgotten and it does not play any role in the modern studies on Augustine. There is still a strong tendency to see the Augustinian doctrine of grace as a doctrine that is certainly somewhat excessive, but which represents the love and mercy of God. The moral price that this contingent concept of grace entails is then bypassed, whereas in fact Augustine created a moral vacuum that is probably visible in his concept of the image of God, which is a man. This moral vacuum is one of the most frightening heritages of Augustinian theology and it seems highly probable that Augustine was well aware of the problem he created. The tension that now and then emerges in his books shows how he wrestled with his conclusions. He was caught in the struggle between the need to be forgiven, to be saved, and the need to create the possibility of moral behaviour. He could only save the latter by making God the ultimate ground of the Good, which He could grant human beings, but only in an absolute, arbitrary way. Hence, He became himself a moral vacuum.

Love and knowledge

A first step, then, in this courageous approach of the divinity creating its own understanding is Augustine's focus on love. In short, the only possible way of knowing God is by loving Him, and this love must be a faithful one (*per fidem diligatur*[39]). Why *faithful* love? Because the role of faith is indispensable in purifying the love with which God will be known. Thus it aims at avoiding any possible confusion with a love for corporeal realities. We will not expand on this aspect of purification; what matters is that love is the first

---

[38] One of the rare exceptions is the critical analysis of the Augustinian ethics given by Miles Hollingworth. Cp. Miles Hollingworth, 'Augustine and the Codes of Life', in, Barry David, ed., *Passionate Mind: Essays in Honor of John M. Rist*, Academia Verlag 2019, 393–414.
[39] *De Trin.* VIII,4,6.

entrance to knowledge. Love, argues Augustine, is not something that all of a sudden pops up; on the contrary, it bears in it something already known. In other words, one cannot love what one did not know previously in some way or another: how can one love what one does not know?[40] This is one of the main arguments in this part of *De Trinitate*: there is no knowledge that in a certain way was not already present, as Augustine will argue at length in book X. Knowledge's structure, therefore, transcends the temporal divides of past and present. It is always actual knowledge, yet it was partly already present before the present. In book VIII, faith is called out to purify this knowledge, but that does not affect the epistemological structure Augustine is developing. Now, if knowledge were already present and needs to be remembered, then, unsurprisingly, memory would be one of the most important aspects of the knowledge that transcends the divide between past and present. Memory concerns the past, but it acts in the present. A simple example is the recollection the author has of Carthage, an example he already used in the *Confessions*. He demonstrates, both in the *Confessions* and in *De Trinitate*, that memory is composed of images (*imagines*), which are the basics of memory. At a certain moment in one's life, they have been collected by our memory and whenever memory needs them again, it will pick them up.[41] However, in *De Trinitate*, the example has become more complicated. Indeed, the author has retained some images of Carthage in his mind, but these are now called *phantasma* or *phantasia*,[42] revealing that the images do not necessarily correspond to the truth, but act as a kind of awakening of Carthage's reality.[43] This even goes for a city the author has never visited; he has an idea of how Alexandria may look, based on what he has heard about this city. Once again, whatever this image may be – even if it is based on hearsay and therefore sometimes

---

[40]*De Trin.* VIII,4,6: *sed quis diligit quod ignorat.* Cp. VIII,5,8: *quo etiam nondum notum deum diligamus?*
[41]*Conf.* X,16,25.
[42]*De Trin.* VIII,6,9. A comparable use of the example of cities one has seen or not is to be found in *De Trin.* XIII,3,6, where Augustine compares Constantinople and Rome. On the 'phantasmatic' aspect of images, see, Isabelle Bochet, 'Le statut de l'image dans la pensée augustinienne', *Archives de Philosophie* 72(2009) 249–69.
[43]*De Trin.* VIII,6,9.

true, sometimes false – it functions as a sound that awakens a certain reality. Even if one has never been to Alexandria, one can still verify whether these images are correct or not. Although the examples of Carthage and Alexandria may differ – one being based on real memories, the other on imagined images – there is a great similarity between them. In both cases, there is a memory – either in one's mind or in the mind of others – that allows us to know whether the images are correct or not. They represent some sort of sign, functioning as a language and trying to reflect a reality they cannot always grasp. Now, this example can be applied to the inner structure of our mind. When we speak about justice, about a just man, the only possibility of doing so is because there must be an interior knowledge of justice. Even if one is not able to be just oneself, one still recognizes the just and the right. It is precisely in the following phrase '*Illud mirabile ut apud se animus videat quod alibi nusquam vidit, ipsum verum iustum animum videat, et sit ipse animus et non sit iustus animus quem apud se ipsum videt*'.[44] In other words, there must be some form of memory allowing us to recognize justice and hence to know it.

In fact, the verb 'to know' does not really correspond to the reality of what we are discussing; we should rather speak of 'loving'. That is what Augustine emphasizes in this whole passage. Indeed, when we speak about justice, truth and the good, knowledge is rather a matter of loving. This is because our mind must turn to the good and just, and this turning, *conversio* (we are still in the platonic scheme)[45] is not a neutral change of direction; no, it is nothing other than loving. This is particularly the case when one thinks of justice. One loves it, and if one loves people who seem to be righteous people, it will be because either they are just or intend to be so. In its purest form, knowledge – particularly, when it comes to objects such as justice and God – can be nothing other than loving. There is more; this is also the way Augustine refers, again, to the self-referential character of love. He will do so in a more extensive way in subsequent books, but the bishop argues here that if one loves a right man, this must be out of love for justice itself. Hence, even if we are not just ourselves but still love the right man,

---

[44]*De Trin.* VIII,6,9.
[45]*De Trin.* VIII,3,5.

this love must a love that is already present. Otherwise, there would be no possibility of loving justice without being just.[46] Augustine will therefore continue to use the verb 'to love' as an equivalent of knowing. However, this 'loving' aspect of knowledge only stresses the double-sided nature of knowledge. It remains something that was already present, and this particular aspect is only reinforced by its similarity to love, for love also possesses a past that becomes present. Indeed, no love is possible unless one somehow already knew what is loved; one can only love what is known.[47] Knowledge, therefore – even when it is considered to be the equivalent of love – has a double character: it is absent and present at the same time. Again, this also goes for love; one can love God but it can also be a love that has been 'forgotten': *sero te amavi*, or late, I loved thee! So 'time' seems to be one of the building blocks Augustine uses to develop his trinitarian epistemology. Yet one of the other axes that seems no less important remains the distinction between right and wrong. Knowledge can be wrong, mistaken, and the same goes for love; it can be erroneous when it turns itself to lower, corporeal, realities. All these aspects matter, and Augustine will explore them in the next books. His starting point here has now been defined, however; he will base himself on the argument that one cannot know something that was not already known previously, a theme he continues to expand in book X. This, then, will be the chorus line: one cannot know or love something that was not known previously.

The image as the cradle of love and knowledge

Indeed, this chorus line will be repeated many times, as if Augustine fears that his reader might forget what must be kept in

---

[46]*De Trin.* VIII,6,9.
[47]Cp. Anne-Isabelle Bouton-Touboulic, 'Qu'il n'y a pas d'amour sans connaissance: étude d'un argument du De Trinitate, livres VIII–XV', in Emmanuel Bermon, Gerald O'Daly, eds., *Le De Trinitate de Saint Augustin, Exégèse, logique et noétique*, Paris 2012, 181–203.

mind. Yet, although this seems superfluous, it is understandable nevertheless. The reader already knows, or at least he can foresee, what the outcome of this whole exercise will be, namely that God is somewhere present in our lives, in our minds and souls, and that love, in the end, is unthinkable without the divine presence; moreover, self-knowledge is impossible without knowledge of God. However, if self-knowledge is not possible without knowledge of God and if, secondly, all knowledge is based on prior knowledge, the conclusion can only be, once again, that God must be present in our lives, even before we realize He is. There must indeed be a part of eternity shedding light on the temporal. There must be a power uniting the divine and the human, creating bridges where no one would have expected them to be. Next, if this starting point is correct, then this 'prior knowledge' should also include the mind's knowledge of itself. There must also be some prior knowledge inside the mind, as the mind is the centre of all our knowledge. It is the mill grinding everything that presents itself as 'knowledge'. The mind in particular must hold onto the chorus line that it is impossible to love what is not known beforehand.[48] Now, this can be shown in the following way. What is already present as the representation of an old memory, sometimes forgotten, sometimes remembered, can only be an image. That is one of the major discoveries Augustine made. If knowledge has qualities that not only concern the present but also the past, and if knowledge is therefore always something that is simultaneously remembered and present, then knowledge must be composed of many images – not only corporeal images but also images of a spiritual and metaphysical reality. Image, knowledge (*intellectus*) and memory[49] depend one on another and image can be seen as the self-referential character of knowledge. The same goes, of course, for love. Once love has taken the place of knowledge, it depends no less on memory and image than knowledge. To love someone or something is to remember someone or something and to have a spiritual image in mind. Therefore, the notion of 'prior' knowledge, of knowledge that was already present, is an extremely

---

[48] *De Trin.* X,1,1: *nam quod quisque prorsus ignorat, amare nullo pacto potest.*
[49] One of the many variations Augustine introduces in order to understand the self-unfolding of the Trinity. The many others comprise e.g. *memoria, intelligentia, voluntas; mens, verbum amor; mens, notitia, amor.*

important one. It shows how every aspect of knowledge is linked to memory and image. Now, if this is correct, is it then also correct to apply this principle of 'prior knowledge' to the mind itself? Yes, it is. The mind loves to know, therefore, it knows what knowledge is. But how should it be able to long for knowledge if it does not understand and know itself? Indeed, it is rightly in this question that we can find our answer. The mind knows itself as longing for knowledge. If it realizes that it is longing, it knows itself. To put this in a short formula: once it seeks to know itself, it knows it is seeking; hence it knows itself.[50] There is a memory of the self before this self had entered the realm of knowledge. In other words, there must also be an image of this self that reminds us of our self before we can even understand it. Moreover, this knowledge concerns the entire mind because knowing something implies knowing it entirely.[51] Of course, although the mind knows itself, and although knowledge is based on prior knowledge, not everything will fall into the category of being known previously. For instance, it is quite possible to love to know the unknown (*amare scire incognita*), something that really cannot be known previously.[52] However, in that particular case, one is confronted with the love of knowing as

---

[50] *De Trin.* X,3,5: *deinde cum quaerit ut noverit, quaerentem se iam noverit. Iam se ergo novit.* It is the first step towards the so-called *Augustinian cogito*, which we can find in detail in *De Trin.* X,10,14 and in *De Civ.* XI,26. Cp on this famous discovery of one's own existence the very detailed and instructive book of Emmanuel Bermon, *Le Cogito dans la pensée de Saint Augustin*, Paris 2001. Regarding the Plotinian background of this argument, one may refer to Enn. V,3, where Plotinus develops an argument that is comparable to the Augustinian one. Cp. Sara Rappe, 'Self-knowledge and Subjectivity in the *Enneads*', in Lloyd P. Gerson, ed., *The Cambridge Companion to Plotinus*, Cambridge 1996, 250–74. However, I do not agree with Rappe on the idea that this is the start of a Western Tradition turning to subjectivism in a Cartesian way. Cp. Mateusz Strózynski, 'There is No Searching for the Self: Self-knowledge in Book X of Augustine's De Trinitate', *Phronesis* 58(2013) 280–300, who strongly rejects the idea of a cartesian 'self'; see note 17 of his article.
[51] *De Trin.* X,4,6.
[52] That is Augustine's objection against the platonic doctrine of memory, as applied in the Meno. *De Trin.* XII,15,24, where he explains that the example of the slave recalling geometrical patterns cannot be correct as not everyone has studied geometry in any earlier life: *non enim omnes in priore vita geometrae fuerunt.*

such, instead of knowing something. When it comes to knowing something, it is impossible to love the unknown.[53]

To conclude, the mind knows itself – although even in its quest for knowledge there is an element of loving to know the unknown. All this seems to be logical; nevertheless, questions may arise. The mind can be wrong about itself and have erroneous ideas about its nature. How can that be explained? Well, no one will be surprised to discover that the reason for these errors can be found in the mind's cupidity. Cupidity is also a form of remembering, and the dynamics of knowing something that in a way was already known is still preserved. This time, what is remembered are only the images that belong to the corporeal world, images that do not direct one's mind to a higher being but only to worlds of a lower nature. Cupidity therefore acts as the perverted form of longing, as a curiosity that cannot be satisfied or quenched, but that tends to cling to some external beauty, some physical objects, of which it preserves the images and then loves them.[54] It even loves them to the point where it thinks of itself as a kind of body because it identifies itself with the images it has kept inside itself.[55] Now, this is a complication we meet inside love. On the one hand, love seems to be grafted on the dynamics of a Trinity unfolding itself and producing its own understanding. As such, it seems to be the self-referential aspect of divine reality. On the other hand, love can also suffer from other dynamics which are less divine. It can turn itself to corporeal objects and easily forget about the divine quality it possesses in itself. In turning itself to this lower reality it is seduced by images, and hence images are at the heart of what love can be: either divine or mean and low. Once again, we meet the structure of similarity (with the divine) and dissimilarity. Memory does not allow us to leave this *bifrons ratio* (*Sol.* II,10,158) behind us.

At the centre of this ambiguity is the tendency not to strive towards a higher reality but to be driven by cupidity, which must be the role of the image. This time, it is not the image taken as the reflection of the self, but rather the image as the enticing reflection of a reality that must be fled. It is an image that haunts the mind

---

[53]*De Trin.* X,1,3.
[54]*De Trin.* X,8,11.
[55]*De Trin.* X,5,7–6,8.

and soul, representing as it were the ever returning Echo that has to be fled. That is the first observation to be made. We are dealing here with images, kept in memory, that are so bewitching that the mind cannot resist them. Nonetheless, as bewitching and enticing as they may be, these images are erroneous and represent the *aversio* (*avertitur ab eo*[56]) from God. Hence, the mind's knowledge of itself turns out to be an erroneous one as it is based on images that may be highly seductive, but that represent a lower reality. Implicitly one can understand that the 'good' image will therefore be an image that turns humans to God in a movement of *conversio*. Moreover, one is already offered a glimpse of Augustine's final conclusion, to be reached in book XIV,14,18, that the ultimate knowledge of oneself must include knowledge of God. However, we are not yet there, since there is still a lot to say about image and memory. The provisional conclusion at this point, however, must be that once a perverted love has made its entrance, the mind changes its attitude and images become twisted. Dissimilarity, when it comes to the divine, increases. It is the moment that cupidity has become such an overwhelming force that nothing in our normal reality can remain what it was. Cupidity turns our minds to a terrestrial beauty that is like a kind of glue, holding the mind back from its ultimate goal: the spiritual reality. Alas, this is not simply a theoretical possibility, but the result of the Fall, and in that sense, it cannot be avoided. Theoretically the mind does not include falsehood (and images certainly do not), but in practice, it cannot exclude it. Once this perversion has entered the scene, love can be wrong, images can be delusive and memory can preserve images we should no longer care for. Augustine is frightened by the power such perverted images can exercise, particularly when it comes to sex, which leads him to quote the example of a man who ejaculated because before his eyes he had a most enticing image of a beautiful woman.[57] This perfectly illustrates the power of images, which can be compared to a kind of clothes that are difficult to take off. In short, there is a large part of our reality that is incompatible with the divine reality we should care about.

---

[56]*De Trin.* X,5,7.

[57]*De Trin.* XI,4,7. The example is in fact a recurrent one. One meets it also in e.g. *De Gen. ad Litt.* XII,15,31; *Conf.* X,30,41; *Sol.* I,10,17.

The double nature of images due to the will

In sum, the divine reality creates its own understanding and the most perfect illustration of this unfolding is the dynamics of love. Yet love itself can become perverted and it then represents a turning away from God, the *aversio*. However, it can also represent the ultimate nature of the divinity itself and its relation with humans. Concerning the latter, if humans are struck by this ultimate divine reality and if they turn their minds to it, they are caught up in the movement of *conversio*, conversion. In both cases, however, the role of images is a primordial one; they represent what was already present. Images can be gateways to the divine reality, they can even be part of it as an integral part of the disclosure of the godhead, but they can also function as bait, leading one's mind to a lower reality. That is what Augustine attempts to sort out in this second part of *De Trinitate* and he continues to do so in book XI. Expanding on the possibility of external similarities with the Trinity, he describes in detail how the corporeal world is seen by our senses, how it then becomes a vision of what was seen, and how it is finally stored in our memories. These images, he warns his readers, can be extremely powerful. Our will can focus so strongly on these images of the corporeal world (which have evidently become interior images in the meantime) that our mind is incapable of distinguishing between the image of the real, outer world, or the image of an invented world.[58] One might say in that sense that images never represent a stable phenomenon; they constantly change and their character can vary accordingly. Images we see in our dreams can be an example of such 'changing' images as they represent corporeal realities but in a twisted form. Augustine then concludes that these images become more powerful and more realistic, to the extent that either fear or desire can be recognized as their products.[59] He depicts a rather

---

[58]*De Trin.* X,4,7: *nec ipsa ratio discernere sinatur utrum foris corporis ipsum uideatur an intus tale aliquid cogitetur.*

[59]*De Trin.* XI,4,7: *Itaque aut metus aut cupiditas quanto vehementior fuerit, tanto expressius formatur acies, sive sentientis ex corpore quod in loco adiacet, sive cogitantis ex imagine corporis quae memoria continetur.*

pessimistic scene of what such an imagination can produce: it is, alas, not a form of creativity, of the mind producing new forms; unfortunately image is not only the power showing how the divinity unfolds itself in multiple ways, but also the scene of men's mind and of his will, which are no longer capable of resisting the attractiveness of corporeal beauty. It is a slippery slope – and not the creative spirit of an author or painter. It is therefore impossible to identify these triadic structures (*memoria, visio, voluntas*[60]) in an undeniable way with the divine reality; the possibility of a destructive tendency can never be excluded. Yet, the Augustinian arguments are not only pessimistic. He did not opt, in dealing with memory and image, for a sole emphasis on dissimilarity; he undoubtedly opted for a relationship that cannot be lost. For, as God created all things good, there must remain a certain similitude with the Good. So, if the soul acts according to its nature, then it acts rightly and orderly; if it becomes vicious, it will act in a sordid and perverted way. Augustine's vocabulary here is incredibly strong[61] and far removed from any subtlety. But it is still the vocabulary based on the model of participation: the relationship cannot be lost. If something is good, it can only be so because it bears in it the stamp of its Creator and even though the distance between Creator and creation can be large, there remains this fragmentary similitude. However, it is not a very optimistic vision. Augustine stresses the gigantic distance that characterizes the relationship between God and man. The only positive aspect he mentions is the fact that man, even when he is caught up in sin, sins because the deepest motive of sinning itself is to be like God, to be His similitude. So even if the image behaves as a distorted one, it does so only because it wants to be a pure image. What, then, is a pure image? This is an image that knows of no nature between itself and God: *nulla interjecta natura est*.[62] That is the ideal image: an image where no one can see the difference between the original and its reflection. However, normally speaking, this is not the case and one can imagine that this picture radically undermines the idea of a Trinity of love, unfolding itself in a new form called 'understanding'. There is very little love

---

[60]*De Trin.* XI, 3,6.
[61]*De Trin.* XI,5,8: *si autem vitiosam, utique turpem atque perversam.*
[62]*De Trin.* XI,5,8.

to be discovered in these lines, unless there is an image that entirely meets the requirements of *nulla natura interjecta* – which will be, of course, none other than the Son.

Yet, there is more to discover. Within the trinitarian structure Augustine is examining, *memoria, visio, voluntas*, he observes a complex interplay between the will and memory. It is the will that in fact takes the lead and transforms certain aspects of memory. This is a new step in his analysis. He started with knowledge and memory, and then introduced love. Next, he went further with image, and now he adds the will. This steeped analysis, difficult to understand, must be clearly kept in mind. Now, speaking about the will, Augustine argues that when a person does not want to listen to another, they can boldly state that they cannot remember what the other has said. This, in fact, is not a matter of remembering, but a matter of will. Their will did not focus on what the other was telling them, and therefore nothing entered their memory.[63] If, on the contrary, our will registers what has been seen and stocks these images into our memory, an interplay still exists between will and memory. We see a sun that is red and round, yet one can imagine, as a kind of weird fantasy, a sun that looks like a green cube. In that sense, images do not have a limit. They are countless[64] and as they are countless, they can be considered the expression of our thinking, which in its turn is structured, this time by the will. It is an infinity created by ourselves. That is how our memory functions when we consider it in terms other than that a storehouse, as it may have seemed in *Confessions*. No, Augustine mentions quite clearly that memory is our way of thinking: *in memoria est congitandi modus*,[65] and it is even cutting-edge thinking: *memoria vero acies cogitantis*.[66] Memory and thinking are indeed closely related, but perhaps the will is even more linked to memory, as Augustine observes when he mentions the example of someone we seemingly have not heard when in reality we did not want to hear them. In that sense, the will unfolds itself into memory and memory unfolds itself into thinking. We then finally find the idea of a reality creating its own understanding. For that reason, there is also room to argue that some creativity must be present

---

[63] *De Trin.* XI,8,15.
[64] *De Trin.* XI,8,12.
[65] *De Trin.* XI,8,14.
[66] *De Trin.* XI,8,14.

in our thinking; there is no limit to the number of representations we can create. No one can stop our imagination.[67] Indeed, there is no limit – there is infinity, but there is also a certain selection. Not everything is retained in memory and that is why Augustine links memory to *measure*. As visions are countless, though at the same time not everything is seen or can be seen, vision is linked to the notion of *number*. Finally, the will is linked to the notion of *weight* because it focuses on certain objects whilst leaving others behind. These then are the names of the trinitarian structure Augustine maintains: *measure*, *number* and *weight*. However, does all this help us to understand the difficult role of the image?

Augustine tries to be clear but the number of subtleties he introduces can be rather confusing. Returning to the notion of the image, it is clear that the divine image in man can only be situated in his soul, his mind. Nothing corporeal should be included in the idea of the divine image as this would be contrary to the idea the image reflecting a superior reality[68]: it should not. In reality, however, this divine image (and this certainly is a kind of sidestep) unifies the different aspects and qualities of the human mind, like the union between man and woman. One part turns towards the superior reality, while another is more interested in earthly matters. Nevertheless, the image still remains a unity and, in that sense, it can be compared to the marital union of man and woman. Of course, the role of the feminine part is more earthly than the masculine, whereas the masculine aspect is visible in the longing for a higher reality,[69] which perfectly corresponds to the distinction between wisdom (*sapientia*) and knowledge (*scientia*). It is clear that the first has the greater merits, and when the apostle explains that we have to be renewed, this can only concern the most elevated aspects of our beings, namely our spiritual mind. One might have thought that Augustine creates a new kind of unity between earthly desires and spiritual longing, but he does not. It is a unity that must be renewed, because as Adam and Eve sinned, their unity must also be renewed. The story of the Fall returns, still with the same explanation: our mind loves its own power and therefore turns away from the general good, focusing

---

[67] *De Trin.* XI,10,17.
[68] *De Trin.* XII,7,12.
[69] *De Trin.* XII,7,10.

now on its own particular interests.[70] The mind originally had an intermediate position; it had its place between heaven and earth, between the corporeal and terrestrial world. The best would be to turn to the spiritual world, whereas the worst would be to turn to the terrestrial. In the latter case, the mind can be said to have left its intermediate position and fallen into the trap of corporeal pleasures. The mind might do so because, focusing on its own interests, it proves to be extremely proud of itself, which can be considered the beginning of all sinning. In reality, the mind should only be attentive to return to its Creator, which is the original way one has to go.[71] If, on the contrary, one prefers to look for corporeal pleasures, then the mind might think that the divine is situated in the images of such physical objects. If, instead, one turns to the One that has created the divine image in human beings, this will be the only acceptable way of living. By doing so, man will cling more to God and less to his own interests.[72] This turn is not only the wish to concentrate on one's own interest, however, it is also the wish to be like God. Now, if the wish to be godlike is also an explanation of the Fall, then this can be interpreted as one of the possible manifestation of one's own interests. The Fall proves to be a complicated story, but it remains a story that does not explain what should be explained. The twofold structure of our being, the connection between similarity and dissimilarity, the Augustinian hesitations: these still remain.

The image turning to itself: The perversion of self-reference

The question now is where we are to find the origin of the ambivalence of the image. What makes the will quiver and doubt the choices to be made? We have already concluded that the story of hereditary sin does not suffice, it is a makeshift explanation that does not work.

---

[70] *De Trin.* XII, 9,14: *potestatem quippe suam diligens anima a communi universo ad privatam partem prolabitur.*
[71] *De Trin.* XII,10,15: *velut viam redeuntes carpimus.* The 'way back' is of course a purely platonic motive. At the same time it reminds the story of the Prodigal Son.
[72] *De Trin.* XII,11,16: *Tanto magis itaque inhaeretur deo quanto minus diligitur proprium.*

Now, surprisingly, two observations in book XII can be considered interesting and innovative approaches. These are approaches that, unexpectedly, do not depend on the notion of the Fall. What makes these observations so surprising? Well, to put it in philosophical terms, they refer to a certain contingency that is absent in the notion of hereditary sin. Contingency seems to be an element that includes a choice, a kind of free will. Pride, for instance, can show itself but it can also disappear. It can be the beginning of sin, but it can also refrain from it. The same goes for a focus on one's own interests: there is a possibility that, time and again, one will look after one's own business[73] – one may even love it, although required to hate it. However, there is also the possibility that one is looking elsewhere, at a higher reality, and is not very much interested in his own affairs. Augustine does state that the divine image can be completely obscured by a greedy mind that prefers its own interest, which means that the mind is returning to itself. This is the returning contradiction: the mind must return to itself in order to find God, but at the same time, when it only refers to itself, it becomes a perverted mind, clinging to persuasive images. The following passage is worth quoting:

> *For the soul loving its own power, slips onwards from the whole which is common, to a part, which belongs especially to itself. And that apostatizing pride, which is called the beginning of sin, whereas it might have been most excellently governed by the laws of God, if it had followed Him as its ruler in the universal creature, by seeking something more than the whole, and struggling to govern this by a law of its own, is thrust on, since nothing is more than the whole, into caring for a part; and thus by lusting after something more, is made less; whence also pride is called the root of all evil. And it administers that whole, wherein it strives to do something of its own against the laws by which the whole is governed, by its own body, which it possesses only in part; and so being delighted by corporeal forms and motions, because it has not the things themselves within itself, and because it is wrapped up in their images, which it has*

---

[73]Cp. Sophie Boagaert, Etienne Kern and Anne Kern-Boquel, *Les énigmes du moi. Saint Augustin. Les Confessions (livre X), Musset, Lorenzaccio, Leiris*, L'Âge d'homme, Paris 2008.

fixed in the memory, and is foully polluted by fornication of the phantasy, while it refers all its functions to those ends, for which it curiously seeks corporeal and temporal things through the senses of the body, either it affects with swelling arrogance to be more excellent than other souls that are given up to the corporeal senses, or it is plunged into a foul whirlpool of carnal pleasure.[74]

First of all, let me make a remark concerning the vocabulary. In this passage Augustine uses the term *anima* as the subject of the whole process of decline. Elsewhere he prefers the term *mens* (mind) or *animus* (spirit). All of these words seem to be different from the notion of image and indeed they cannot be considered synonyms. Yet, there is considerable overlap. *Imago* is in fact the essential quality of the *mens*, the *anima* or *animus*. It is a special quality making the human mind a particular entity and, in that sense, it can be regarded as the equivalent of soul,[75] mind or spirit. When Augustine says that the mind loses the divine image, it means nothing other than having said that the divine image was ruining and losing itself. The divine image is not comparable to a kind of external object, something that does not belong to the mind but that is only owned by it. No, the divine image is the most essential quality of the mind and the mind cannot be conceived of without this quality. Next, in this passage, Augustine insists on the egotistical behaviour of the soul in case it renounces its true nature. In that case, it is interested in itself in a perverted way; it does not focus on the universal but on the particular. Now, if the soul is

---

[74]*De Trin.* XII,9,14: *Potestatem quippe suam diligens anima, a communi universo ad privatam partem prolabitur, et apostatica illa superbia, quod initium peccati dicitur, cum in universitate creaturae Deum rectorem secuta, legibus eius optime gubernari potuisset, plus aliquid universo appetens, atque id sua lege gubernare molita, quia nihil est amplius universitate, in curam partilem truditur, et sic aliquid amplius concupiscendo minuitur, unde et avaritia dicitur radix omnium malorum; totumque illud ubi aliquid proprium contra leges, quibus universitas administratur, agere nititur, per corpus proprium gerit, quod partiliter possidet; atque ita formis et motibus corporalibus delectata, quia intus ea secum non habet, cum eorum imaginibus, quas memoriae fixit, involvitur, et phantastica fornicatione turpiter inquinatur, omnia officia sua ad eos fines referens, quibus curiose corporalia ac temporalia per corporis sensus quaerit, aut tumido fastu aliis animis corporeis sensibus deditis esse affectat excelsior, aut coenoso gurgite carnalis voluptatis immergitur.* Translation, Nicene and Post-Nicene Fathers I,III, slightly altered.
[75]Cp. *De Gen. ad Litt.* III,20,31.

interested in itself, this implies that it is referring to itself. It seeks its completion and its pleasure in itself. Of course it has to refer to itself but, by doing so, choices have to be made – either to resemble the original divine reality as its faithful image or to focus on the self as an independent reality.

This self-reference is a striking motive as well as a critical one. It raises the question of whether self-reference of the soul, endowed with a divine image, is nevertheless compatible with different realities. Is it indeed kind of free choice? This is at least what is suggested in the Plotinian philosophy, where self-reference is not reduced to making oneself the norm and boundary of all reality, but where it has to do with un unfolding character of a unique reality that wants to create its own self-understanding. If this were a possibility, then the image could have a constantly changing and different outlook. Indeed it could turn to the highest reality, the divine one, but also to a 'lower' one, as Augustine would qualify it. Then again, if we look at the notion of the image itself, is such a self-referential character of an image possible? Can or should an image – let alone the *divine* image – refer to itself? Logically, at least, this seems impossible. Normally speaking an image should refer to something else – that of which it is the image – and this is what Augustine continually emphasizes. The divine image refers to its Creator, and its commandment is to remain related to the Creator by its acts, thoughts, desires and so on. There is no other way an image can function; it always refers to something from which it has been derived, but which exists outside the image it created. The image should therefore only refer to its divine origin and never to itself and its multiple realities. Augustine himself evoked, as we have seen, a portrait, which represents a man but will never be identical with the person whose image it refers. There is a distinction, even separation, between the image and the original and, although they belong to each other, they can never be reduced one to another. So, apparently, an image should never refer to itself. A photograph will not refer to itself and if any image ever did so, it would create a one-dimensional concept of the image. It would no longer refer to an original, to the Creator: it would be Narcissus looking at himself. It would create a world in which Narcissus has fled the referential context, refusing to listen to anything other than his own desires. Reality would no longer be an interplay between phenomena and their interpretation, it would simply be the vicious circle of a subject repeating itself in a void universe. At least, that is what it looks like at first glance.

The image turning to itself: More than perversion

Or should we say things are more complicated? Augustine uses important arguments several times based on the idea of self-reference. He does so in the case of knowledge and love, and we will shortly return to these arguments. The most important aspect of these arguments should not be overlooked, however. Once Augustine starts to base himself on self-referential arguments and once he introduces the turn of the image to a lower reality as a self-referential character, there is no longer any need to consider the divine reality as the sole relation possible between the image and the reality it refers to. Nevertheless, this is what he tries to do in his self-referential arguments on knowledge and love. Both are to be regarded as the unfolding – albeit imperfect – of the divine reality. Once self-referentiality can also be applied to the turn to a lower reality, however, the divine reality is only one option among many others. Augustine thought this might accord him some decisive arguments in favour of the divine aspect of the image possessed by the human mind but, on the contrary, the image proved to be a creative quality of the human mind, which turned itself to whichever reality it found interesting. That reality could be the divine reality, but it could also be any other one. Self-reference does not entail the necessity of a divine origin to the image; it creates the contingency of choices no one could foresee. Let us, therefore, have a closer look at these two arguments concerning self-reference, one dealing with knowledge and the other with love.

The first argument then is that Augustine tried hard to prove that the mind must know itself. His argument was the observation that, once the mind realizes it is longing for knowledge, it knows itself.[76] In other words: once it realizes that it remembers that it remembers, it knows itself. It even loves itself, as this longing for knowledge is nothing other than an ardent love. As Augustine states in some beautiful lines:

> What then does the mind love, when it seeks ardently to know itself, whilst it is still unknown to itself? For, behold, the mind seeks to behold itself, and is excited thereto by studious zeal. It

---

[76]*De Trin.* X,3,5; X,10,14.

loves, therefore, but what does it love? Is it itself? But how can this be when it does not yet know itself and no one can love what he does not know? ... Or when it loves to know itself, does it love, not itself, which it does not yet know, but the very act of knowing; and feel the more annoyed that itself is wanting to its own knowledge wherewith it wishes to embrace all things? And it knows what it is to know; and whilst it loves this, which it knows, desires also to know itself. Whereby then, does it know its own knowing, if it does not know itself? For it knows that it knows other things, but that it does not know itself; for it is from hence that is knows also what knowing is. In what way, then, does that which does not know itself, know itself as knowing anything? For it does not know that some other mind knows, but that itself does so. Therefore it knows itself. Further, when it seeks to know itself, it knows now itself as seeking. Therefore again it knows itself. And hence it cannot altogether not know itself, when certainly it does so far know itself as that it knows itself as not knowing itself. But it does not know itself not to know itself. And therefore, in the very fact that it seeks itself, it is clearly convicted of being more known to itself than unknown. For it knows itself as seeking and as not knowing itself, in that it seeks to know itself.[77]

That is it: the answer is that the mind knows itself thanks to the discovery of a self-referential dynamic, of a self-referential character that has different aspects. For example, the mind can doubt its own existence, as Augustine shows in X,10,14, but it must also admit that it still remembers its own doubts, although this doubt has no

---

[77]*De Trin.* X,3,5: *Quid ergo amat mens, cum ardenter se ipsam quaerit ut noverit, dum incognita sibi est? Ecce enim mens semetipsam quaerit ut noverit, et inflammatur hoc studio*[5]. *Amat igitur: sed quid amat? Si se ipsam, quomodo, cum se nondum noverit, nec quisquam possit amare quod nescit? ... An cum se nosse*[9] *amat, non se quam nondum novit, sed ipsum nosse amat; acerbiusque tolerat se ipsum deesse scientiae suae, qua vult cuncta comprehendere? Novit autem quid sit nosse, et dum hoc amat quod novit, etiam se cupit nosse. Ubi ergo nosse suum novit, si se non novit?*[10] *Nam novit quod alia noverit*[11]*, se autem non noverit; hinc enim novit et quid sit nosse. Quo pacto igitur se aliquid scientem scit, quae se ipsam nescit? Neque enim alteram mentem scientem scit, sed se ipsam. Scit igitur se ipsam. Deinde cum se quaerit ut noverit, quaerentem se iam novit. Iam se ergo novit. Quapropter non potest omnino nescire se, quae dum se nescientem scit, se utique scit. Si autem se nescientem nesciat, non se quaeret ut sciat. Quapropter eo ipso quo se quaerit, magis se sibi notam quam ignotam esse convincitur. Novit enim se quaerentem atque nescientem, dum se quaerit ut noverit.*

absolute power. On the contrary, it is transformed into knowledge. Therefore, the self-referential character of the mind seems to be a positive discovery; indeed, in a certain way it is. It creates an approach to oneself that is not based on the observations of others, but that is only based on a logical argument; however, this logical argument does not imply that self-reference only concerns one reality. There is no compulsory conclusion saying that self-reference is nothing other than a vicious circle. Indeed, I can prove my own existence, but that does not imply that my mind only refers to its own existence, excluding other realities. No, it certainly does not. What Augustine, on the contrary, tells us in the above-quoted passage, is that it is impossible to know that one is longing to know oneself without admitting that this knowing of one's longing for the unknown already represents a certain knowledge. In other words, there is a certain contradiction in terms when it comes to knowing the unknown: the unknown regards one's own mind and existence, but as soon as one becomes aware of one's own longing for knowledge, this longing is already part of one's knowledge. Yet the longing can have many objects aside from one's own existence. There is still this unfolding of a many-sided reality that creates its own understanding. Hence, there is no way to conclude that the Augustinian subject, discovering the complex relationship between knowledge and ignorance, is comparable to the Cartesian subject, who definitely separates the subject from the surrounding world. What Augustine means is that, in its quest for knowledge, the mind discovers desire, longing, life, memory, understanding, ignorance and, above all, love. There is no knowledge of oneself without referring to these realms of our inner reality.

Now, one might object that the same goes for Descartes, does it not? Did he not base his whole argument on the notion of doubt? Hence, is it not correct to conclude that authors such as Charles Taylor[78] are right in stating that Augustine represents the beginning of the Western tradition of subjectivism? I could not disagree more, but to be clear

---

[78]Taylor, *Sources of the Self*. Taylor was criticized for his rendering of Augustinian thought, but the influence of his claim that Augustine possesses a proto-Cartesian argument can hardly be underestimated. It is the basis, in Taylor's view of the discovery of the modern 'self'. For criticism on Taylor, cp. David Peddle, 'Re-sourcing Charles Taylor's Augustine', *Augustinian Studies* 32(2001) 207–17; Edward Booth, 'Saint Augustine and the Western Tradition of Self-Knowing', Saint Augustine Lecture 1986, Villanova 1989.

at this point, we should turn to Augustine's argument concerning love and its self-referential character, as he describes it in IX,2,2:

> Well then, when I, who make this inquiry, love anything, there are three things concerned – myself and that which I love, and love itself. For I do not love love, except I love a lover; for there is no love where nothing is loved. Therefore, there are three things – he who loves, and that which is loved and love. But what if I love none except myself? Will there not be then two things – that which I love, and love? For he who loves and that which is loved are the same when anyone loves himself; just as to love and to be loved, in the same way, is the very same thing when any one loves himself. For in that case to love and to be loved are not two different things; just as he who loves and he who is loved are not two different persons. But yet, even so, love and what is loved are still two things. For there is no love when any one loves himself, except when love itself is loved. But it is one thing to love one's self, another to love one's own love. For love is not loved, unless as already loving something; since where nothing is loved there is no love. Therefore there are two things when any one loves himself – love and that which is loved. For then he that loves and that which is loved are one. Whence it seems that it does not follow that three things are to be understood where love is.[79]

Love, at first glance, will mostly concern an external object. One loves someone else, yet there is also of course the possibility of one loving oneself. In the latter case the self-referential character of love

---

[79] *De Trin.* IX,2,2,: *Ecce ego qui hoc quaero, cum aliquid amo tria sunt: ego, et quod amo, et ipse amor. Non enim amo amorem, nisi amantem amem; nam non est amor, ubi nihil amatur. Tria ergo sunt: amans, et quod amatur, et amor. Quid, si non amem nisi me ipsum? Nonne duo erunt: quod amo, et amor? Amans enim et quod amatur, hoc idem est, quando se ipse amat; sicut amare et amari, eodem modo idipsum est cum se quisque amat. Eadem quippe res bis dicitur, cum dicitur: 'Amat se', et: 'amatur a se'. Tunc non est aliud atque aliud, amare et amari; sicut non est alius atque alius, amans et amatus. At vero amor, et quod amatur, etiam sic duo sunt. Non enim quisquis se amat amor est nisi cum amatur ipse amor. Aliud est autem amare se, aliud amare amorem suum. Non enim amatur amor, nisi iam aliquid amans; quia ubi nihil amatur, nullus est amor. Duo ergo sunt, cum se quisque amat: amor, et quod amatur. Tunc enim amans et quod amatur unum est. Unde videtur non esse consequens ut ubicumque amor fuerit, iam tria intellegatur.*

will be comparable to the self-referential character of knowledge – albeit that the self-referential character is defined in a slightly different way. Let us nonetheless start with the common case of someone loving someone else. In that case, we have to reckon with the one who loves, then with the beloved and finally with the love that binds the lover and the beloved. Those are the three elements that have to be taken into account. Imagine that one loves oneself. Then, the lover and the one who is loved will be the same. In that particular case, there are only two things left to be reckoned with: the lover and the love, the lover being the same as the one that is loved. That is, at least, what it seems to be, but things are more complicated. The lover is not only the same as the beloved, but one also has to conclude that the lover loves love. Why so? Because love must love something, otherwise there is no love. Once it loves oneself, however, the difference between the beloved and love itself is abolished. Hence, there is indeed the lover and the love, but the lover, once he loves himself, loves nothing other than love itself because it concerns himself. Therefore, one may conclude that love belongs to the subject as well as to the object. That is the brilliant way Augustine introduces the self-referential dynamic in the notion of love. Love can refer to itself and it can do so in an extraordinary way. It is, in the very best tradition of a Plotinian approach, love unfolding itself in a new understanding of what love is. Indeed, it is a beautiful argument, and it represents a new way of considering the self-referential character of love. However, although this is highly innovative, it is of course not the beginning of any subjectivism in the Western tradition. On the contrary, this is the beginning of an interpretation of reality creating its own understanding. In the case of love, it is the beloved becoming love itself. Yet, dealing with love, the conclusion has to be the same as in the case of knowledge: there is no definition of what kind of love is unfolding itself. Of course, I can love myself, but the self we are speaking of has not been defined. Hence, the unfolding character that is included in the notion of love still regards many possible realities.

Regarding the image, then, the conclusion may be obvious. The image is the ultimate unfolding of reality – but this unfolding can have different forms. There is on the one hand a deep understanding, *intellectus*, of the divine reality that reveals itself in the image. This is what Augustine considers the original divine image; the image that can stick to its origin and that reflects the divine reality as truthfully as possible. Yet, while perhaps fully conscious of its origin, this divine image can also turn away from the godhead, with dissimilarity prevailing. There is another way of unfolding, in which our inner divine image turns to a reality that is far from the divine, at least in the eyes of Augustine. For we gather many normal images whilst living our lives: we visit a city, and we retain in our memory the images the city has left in our mind. However, it is not only these rather harmless images that can be stored in our memory, but there are also more seductive images: both are countless, infinite. One can keep in one's mind the images of corporeal pleasures and even want to relive them. Now, it is to these images that the divine image we have in our mind can also turn itself. What happens in this case is that it forgets its divine origin and seeks its pleasure in identifying itself with these lower images. This is a process Augustine describes in detail, which starts with the notion of self-reference. Indeed, the mind is able to remember itself, to love itself and to understand itself.[80] But all this understanding has a twofold character, and it is useless unless one remembers God by whom he has been created. Self-reference can show us the dynamic of an unfolding reality, sure, but it can only do so if the process of unfolding starts at the top of all realities, at the highest reality conceivable. It is only from that ultimate reality that the unfolding can take place. Therefore, knowledge of oneself, love of oneself, can only be conceived of as long as the highest principle is included. In other words, one can only love oneself if one loves God; one can only know oneself once one knows God.[81] It can therefore be said that the one who loves himself without loving God, in fact, hates oneself.[82] Of course, the divine image can never be lost,[83] it has an immortal nature,[84] but it can become utterly forgetful once it has started to identify itself with the lower images. This is a development that can be interpreted as the perversion of the divine image and, of course, it is to be avoided.

---

[80]*De Trin.* XIV,12,15; XIV,14,18.
[81]*De Trin.* XIV,12,15.
[82]*De Trin.* XIV,14,18: *Qui ergo se diligere novit, deum diligit: qui vero non diligit deum, etiam si se diligit, quod ei naturaliter inditum est, tamen non inconvenienter odisse se dicitur.*
[83]*De Trin.* XIV,14,19.
[84]*De Trin.* XIV,4,6.

If, nevertheless, this happens, there will be an absolute necessity to renew one's image. Alas, as a rule, the divine image will indeed have become deformed during one's life and therefore it must always be renewed. It is like leaving behind the 'old man' one once was and taking new clothes, as Augustine explains quoting St. Paul.[85] However, this is a long process and requires a daily exercise in renewal. Even then, this whole process of a constant renewal will only be completed in the life after this life, and it will be then – but only then (!) – that one's image will really resemble the image of the Son.[86] To recover the original divine image that one once was is therefore a long process that can only be achieved with the help of God himself: *without Me, you can't do anything.*[87] The latter aspect is an important one. Augustine insists on the fact that man is only capable of remembering God and turning to Him thanks to God's merciful grace: *nonnisi eius gratuito affectu posse se surgere*, meaning man is only capable of getting himself up thanks to the free love of God.[88] Yet, his drifting apart, his falling, can only be due to his own lack of will. The circle of perfection starts with God and ends with Him. Humans cannot be perfect, although in fact they should only care about the divine image they have received flawlessly.

The conclusion, then, may be that the self-referential character Augustine wanted to lead to the divine reality is in fact the unfolding of many possible realities. Augustine tacitly admits this by the emphasis he places on the necessity of the renewal of our inner image. Of course, our image has a divine origin, but it unfolds many other realities that are perhaps far from being divine in any sense of the word. In Augustine's view, this is due to our sinful nature, which is an argument that allows him to maintain that the image can only have a divine origin. This is the argument that basically draws upon the model of participation, according to which there is no absolute divide between the origin of the image, the Creator and the image itself. On the other hand, as the image can be completely obscured, there is also the model of the mind sinning and turning away from

---

[85] *De Trin.* XIV,16,22; quote of *Col.* 3,9.
[86] *De Trin.* XIV,18,24.
[87] *De Trin.* XIV,17,23, quote of *John* 15,5: *sine me nihil potestis facere.*
[88] *De Trin.* XIV,15,21.

its divine origin. That is the model explaining the absolute divide between the Good of the Creator and the evil that man practices. These models are difficult to harmonize and Augustine mixes them up. This may be understandable, but in that case the following question remains: what can human morality be based on? It is not on man's sinful nature, yet neither is it on the divine origin of the image, as this divine origin can be completely corrupted and as there is no possibility to remedy unless God decides to help.

6

The final question: It's all about language

If this is correct, do we then still have in front of us, in these last books of *De Trinitate*, the ordinary scheme of the twofold approach we have already met? On the one hand there is an absolute divide between the Creator and the creation, a divide that has become unbridgeable due to the Fall. For, as Augustine explains, there is always this inevitable tendency of our mind to turn to a lower reality, to the other images which have nothing to do with divine reality, but which continue to murmur tempting suggestions to one's mind.[1] Yet though the process itself is clearly pictured by Augustine, the 'why' of this process is still not visible. Where does this moral vacuum stem from? Therefore, this first approach adopted by Augustine leaves us still with important yet unresolved questions. On the other hand, there is the Augustinian model built on the notion of participation, which excludes such an absolute divide. Now, it is certainly true that the participation model seems to be very important to Augustine. He even mentions that there is a natural order according to which God is the top of the reality hierarchy; hence, it belongs to the mind's nature to cling to this ultimate reality.[2] This is a concept based on

---

[1] That is the image Augustine pictures in *Conf.* VIII,11,26: *Retinebant nugae nugarum et vanitates vanitantium, antiquae amicae meae, et succutiebant vestem meam carneam et submurmurabant: 'Dimittisne nos?' et: 'A momento isto non erimus tecum ultra in aeternum', et: 'A momento isto non tibi licebit hoc et illud ultra in aeternum'. Et quae suggerebant in eo, quod dixi: 'hoc et illud'.*

[2] *De Trin.* XIV,14,20: *Sic enim ordinata est naturarum ordine, non locorum, ut supra illam non si nisi ille.*

the idea that the mind can participate in God's nature, truth and happiness.³ Yet we cannot avoid a problem similar to the one we met in the first approach, meaning there is no possibility of remembering the divine origin of the image without God's help. Even though the divine image can never be lost, it can only be awakened by God's interference. This comes down to the same question we met in the first approach. Apparently there is a fundamental lack of human capacities that does not allow humans to overcome their weakness. But what, then, is this lack? It is a lack so fundamental that images become puppets in a play without a script.

We have already mentioned that Augustine returns to his old scheme of *similis/dissimilis* in the last book of *De Trinitate*. Extensively using the Pauline metaphor of looking in a mirror as in a mystery (I Cor. 13), the bishop now argues that the mirror can be compared to the divine image and that the mystery is the dark side of this image, meaning our lack of understanding.[4] Taking it from there, Augustine introduces, in a last endeavour to understand the divine reality, the notion of the words in our mind that can reveal a resemblance with the divine Word. Thus, after memory, after image, he finally addresses the notion of words and there we will find his ultimate view on the human and divine reality. For undoubtedly, all our wisdom and our knowledge, all our thoughts, are all based on words. These words then are a kind of image in which we can see the reflection of the divine Word. But it is only a 'kind' of resemblance, a 'kind' of understanding; there still remains a great dissimilarity![5] Of course words are important; there can be no thoughts, no action, without a word that precedes them. But these human words, even though there is much resemblance with the divine Word,[6] can never be identified with it. What, then, is the main resemblance with the divine Word? The fact that our mind is capable of distinguishing between true and false. If our human words exactly reflect our knowledge, then they are

---

[3]*Ibid.: accedente quidem ista ad participationem naturae, Veritatis, et beatitudinis illius.*
[4]*De Trin.* XV,9,16.
[5]*De Trin.* XV,11,20: *Quapropter qui cupit ad qualemcumque similitudinem Verbi Dei, quamvis per multa dissimilem, pervenire.*
[6]*De Trin.* XV,11.20.

capable of separating truth from falsehood.⁷ Secondly, there is also another parallel. The divine Word, being the source of the whole of creation, is mainly a creative force. The same, however, goes for the mental word humans have in their mind. There is nothing humans can create without a mental word being the start of what we do, so indeed, there are important resemblances. Yet, notwithstanding these similarities, the ultimate conclusion is that dissimilarity is inevitable and unsurmountable. Let us examine the following passage, taken from XV, 13,22:

> *This knowledge (i.e. the divine knowledge), therefore, is far unlike our knowledge. And the knowledge of God is itself also His wisdom, and His wisdom is itself His essence or substance. Because in the marvelous simplicity of that nature, it is not one thing to be wise and another to be, but to be wise is to be; as we have often said in earlier books. But our knowledge is in most things capable both of being lost and of being recovered, because to us to be is not the same as to know or to be wise; since it is possible for us to be, even although we know not, neither are wise in that which we have learned from elsewhere. Therefore, as our knowledge is unlike that knowledge of God, so is our word also, which is born from our knowledge, unlike that Word of God which is born from the essence of the Father. And this is as if I should say, born from the Father's knowledge, from the Father's wisdom; or still more exactly, from the Father who is knowledge, from the Father who is wisdom.*⁸

---

⁷*De Trin.* XV,11,20.
⁸*De Trin.* XV,13,22: *Longe est igitur huic scientiae scientia nostra **dissimilis**. Quae autem scientia dei est, ipsa et sapientia; et quae sapientia, ipsa essentia sive substantia. Quia in illius naturae simplicitate mirabili, non est aliud sapere, aliud esse; sed quod est sapere, hoc est et esse, sicut et in superioribus libris saepe iam diximus. Nostra vero scientia in rebus plurimis propterea et amissibilis est et receptibilis, quia non hoc est nobis esse quod scire vel sapere: quoniam esse possumus, etiam si nesciamus, neque sapiamus ea quae aliunde didicimus. Propter hoc, sicut nostra scientia illi scientiae dei, sic et nostrum verbum quod nascitur de nostra scientia, **dissimile** est illi verbo dei quod natum est de patris essentia. Tale est autem ac si dicerem: 'De patris scientia, de patris sapientia'; vel, quod est expressius: 'De patre scientia, de patre sapientia'.* Translation Nice and Post-Nicene Fathers.

In these lines, Augustine uses the word *dissimilis* twice and insists on the difference between our knowledge and the divine one. *Dissimilis* is a word that, after this passage, returns several times and will result in the following phrase: 'there is such a huge dissimilarity between our words and God as well as between our words and the Word of God, though there is some likeness'.[9] Moreover, the image has admittedly been crafted by the Trinity, but it has become perverted due to its own vices. Hence, it can certainly be compared to the Trinity, but one should be aware of the fact that even though it resembles the Trinity, the dissimilarity is fundamental.[10] Thus, the dissimilarity prevails at any moment of man's life, even in the afterlife. For even in the afterlife, though we will be similar to God and though we will see Him as He is, there will still be a vast dissimiliarity.[11]

The loss of language

Why, in fact? That is the final question. In the above-quoted passage there is a glimpse of an answer. Augustine argues that it is the same in God to be wise and to be, which is not the case with humans. In other words, there is a divine simplicity that humans can never attain; our knowledge will always be different from the divine one. The keyword in this passage is of course '*simplicitas*'. God's unity is so unique that everything He is – wise, great, love, merciful – belongs to His being. His love and His being are not two different qualities; they are one and the same. The argument is very much

---

[9] *De Trin.* XV,16,26: *tanta sit nunc in isto aenigmate dissimilitudo dei et verbi dei, in qua tamen nonnulla similitudo comperta est.*

[10] *De Trin.* XV,20,40: *Verum ne hanc imaginem ab eadem trinitati factam, et suo vitio indeterius commutatam, ita eidem comparet trinitati ut omno modo existimet similem; sed potius in qualicumque ista similitudine magnam dissimilitudinem cernat, quantum esse satis videbatur, admonui.*

[11] *De Trin.* XV,11,21: *Cum ergo hac transformatione ad perfectum fuerit haec imago renovata, similes Deo erimus, quoniam videbimus eum, non per speculum, sed sicuti est quod dicit apostolus Paulus, facie ad faciem Nunc vero in hoc speculo, in hoc aenigmate, in hac qualicumque similitudine, quanta sit etiam dissimilitudo, quis potest explicare?*

a Plotinian one and it is often repeated by Augustine, but the consequences of this approach seem to be different in the case of Plotinus and Augustine. In both cases, man can be wise or great, thanks to their participation in wisdom or greatness. However, in the case of Augustine, this participation will never end, and there remains a difference between the One and the Many. Augustine even insists on this eternal difference: the image remains unequal in an incomparable way.[12] What is striking, therefore, is the fact that Augustine does not have any positive view on the Many. The way in which the Many reflect the One and understand it, is necessarily imperfect. There is only one understanding that can be dubbed a perfect one and that is the Son. The Son is the perfect image; He is the complete understanding of the One that is the Father. However, all other images, the human ones, can only be imperfect ones. They represent the Many that can never attain the divine essence. The difference between these two kinds of images is even visible in the vocabulary Augustine uses. He insists on the fact that Christ has indeed adopted the human body but never changed into a human body: *assumendo non consumendo*.[13] The difference is clear: there is of course some similarity between Christ and humans, but this is in fact only a superficial one. The incarnation is not the element that creates real equality between the Son and humans. It is purely Adoptionism, forged in times when Monarchianism was a vital tradition. On the other hand, man cannot become completely similar to God. Hence, regardless of whether one starts at the divine reality or at the human one, there will never be any equality; the dissimilarity will remain forever.

However, this insistence on God's unity and on the fact that His wisdom, His love, His greatness are nothing other than His being, make it impossible to distinguish between all these qualities. Whatever it is, God is it fully, *implying that language, as the means allowing us to differentiate, becomes useless*. Language is the ultimate possibility to differentiate, and it is therefore the ultimate expression of the Many. Yet, if language represents the Many, then speaking about God is an attempt to harmonize the One and the Many. However, this attempt is a kiss of death to language, for

---

[12]*De Trin.* XV,23,43: *incomparabiliter quidem imparem.*
[13]*De Trin.* XV,11,20.

trying to harmonize the One and the Many by means of language is nothing less than to deprive language completely of its sense. For we do not say anything specifically when we say, for instance, that God is wise. There is no difference between His wisdom and His greatness. What then is left when it comes to language? Hardly anything. Language loses its meaning once the difference between, let us say, great, wise and merciful disappears. From that moment on, language becomes a kind of tool that is officially deemed a reflection of the divine reality, yet in reality it can no longer be so once words lose their meaning. Moreover, one would also wonder whether the divine Word still has any particular meaning. If it contains all the perfect qualities the godhead possesses, where does it really become a word, meaning part of language? Indeed, a part of a language, meaning that language always entails a kind of splitting up of every unity. There is a kind of parting of the ways between being and language, dividing the original unity between God and his Word. Language thus becomes a separate reality that has been ripped out of the divine reality because of its multiplicity. Admittedly, one can still argue that our language has been created by the divine Word. Language in this sense is a gift from God, belonging intimately to the image we have been bestowed with. It should reflect the Word that is God Himself. However, this divine Word in itself already has many meanings and this situation only worsens when it comes to human language. So, indeed, human language belongs to the world of the Many; there is no possibility of a univocal truth. Each word has a particular meaning and, dependent on its context, its meaning will change. Of course, it may occasionally resemble the divine Word because both have many meanings, but it will always lack the equality with the divine that the Word possesses. Hence, there is *per definitionem* no absolute equivalence possible between language and thinking, between language and being. Of course, there is a partial equivalence but, understandably, the shortcomings of the equivalence prevail and they do so because language cannot get rid of its multiplicity – and it should not do so! That is exactly the essence of language, the quality that particularly characterizes it: its infinite variety. No word cannot be replaced by another; no word does not take another meaning once the context changes. Words can bow once reality asks them to be flexible. They can take different colours, dependent on whether they have to hide or to show something. They can evoke and suggest realities in a never-ending range. Now, surprisingly, it is in this sense that language is the perfect counterpart to God's infinity. This is what it is: language differs completely from the divine reality but, indeed, there is an unexpected parallel between the divine reality and the human language: *the infinity they both have in common.*

Indeed, this is what it is: the multiplicity of language is not the opposite of God's simplicity. On the contrary, it is a reflection of His simplicity. Of course, multiplicity and simplicity seem to be opposites, they seem to be at odds with one another, but both have an unexpected infinity in common. Language is a universe without any limitation, which also goes for simplicity – at least in the Plotinian sense. Hence, language could be considered a very particular reflection of the divine simplicity. That is the fascinating paradox Augustine could not master. It is the same problem he struggled with when he attempted to analyse the role of memory. The same infinity, memories that are countless and that never stop creating new memories. Dealing with memory, Augustine already met the problem of this infinity, which he could not master unless he linked it to God. Now, the problem becomes even more visible: language and being do have one dimension in common – they both are infinite. Yet harmonizing God and language comes down to a kiss of death of God to language. At the same time, it is a kiss of life: rejecting the infinite possibilities of language by God implies creating a parallel universe. A universe that mirrors His own and which is as infinite as is God's simplicity. Implicitly, Augustine admits so – sometimes overtly, sometimes indirectly – in *De Doctrina Christiana* and *De Magistro*. In particular, in book II of *De Doctrina Christiana* he mentions that an innumerable number of words serve as signs and significations,[14] although the essence of a word cannot be expressed by words.[15] This is something Augustine is quite aware of and he therefore repeats it several times.[16] However, apparently this infinity

---

[14]*De Doctr. Chr.* II,3,4.
[15]*De Doctr. Chr.* II,3,4: Sed innumerabilis multitudo signorum, quibus suas cogitationes homines exerunt, in verbis constituta est. Nam illa signa omnia quorum genera breviter attigi, potui verbis enuntiare, verba vero illis signis nullo modo possem.
[16]*De Doctr. Chr.* II,25,39; *De Mag.* 13,43. Cp. Richard Leo Enos, Roger Thompson et al., *The Rhetoric of St. Augustine of Hippo: De Doctrine Christiana & the Search for a Distinctly Christian Rhetoric*, Waco Texas 2008.

was not what really struck him. Basically, he considers words as signs, and language in general is nothing more than a system that allows us to refer to ultimate reality. He lets the aspect of infinity slip away. It goes as unnoticed as a wave rising and returning into the sea without leaving any trace. Language, to put it quite simply, is nothing more in Augustine's view than the shadow of thinking and being, as he argues in *De Trin.* V,I,1. It is one of the multiple reflections that the highest being produces as a kind of lower reality. Therefore, its use was limited to reflection and reference; it was entirely bound by the reality whose servant it was supposed to be. Language in itself does not have an independent existence; Augustine would never have thought along the lines of language as an independent reality, and such independence is an interpretation that we will only meet in the era of nominalism, centuries later. That is: as Augustine deprived language of its roots, its connection with the ultimate reality, he isolated language as a realm apart. But the status of this realm is highly unclear. However, this is not the conclusion Augustine himself drew. What sufficed in his eyes was to make clear that language is only a reflection of a higher reality. Yet, to be honest, the multiplicity, the infinite richness that belongs to language, provoked his suspicion. He loved language and at the same time he loathed it. Language never voiced something *unisono*, so to speak, and it is precisely this lack of simplicity with which Augustine struggled. Plato already warned that poets and authors were to be distrusted, that Homer was not a poet to be used for any education; Augustine held exactly the same opinion as he explained in *Confessions*.[17] Language had no realm of its own, it was only a province of a very large country where the Sovereign had already decided that only his personal Word could be dubbed his perfect image. Human language, by contrast, was nothing more than a multicoloured picture that sometimes resembles this unique Word, but that sometimes, because of its many colours, is also totally different from this Word. In fact, however, in Augustine's

---

[17] Cp. *Conf.* IX,2,2. On the language of the confession, see, B. Pranger, 'Augustine and the Silence of the Sirens', *Journal of Religion* 91(2011) 64–77; Philip Burton, *Language in the Confessions of Augustine*, Oxford 2007. The way Augustine speaks of Aeneas and the death of Dido, with much contempt, is comparable to the way Plato spoke of Homer. Cp. *Conf.* I,13,20–1.

view it should follow the pattern he had developed for memory: forever linked to the divine reality. Unfortunately, this was not the case; language was a realm apart. It is an ambivalence with which Augustine was uneasy. He, who was an author by vocation, by temperament, by talent, could not accept the fact that the infinite charm of words could never be voiced in an *unisono* way. In that sense, he fought a battle similar to the one Plato had tried to win. Both authors, however, were helpless in front of the power of their own talent and nature. So, of course, Augustine insisted on the inadequacy of language. Language should bring us nearer to God, but in fact it could only be a lesser reflection of the deity. That is the gap Augustine never managed to bridge.[18] There is even more; his own mastery of words and language, his rhetorical skills, they all speak another language than the one Augustine allows them. Even if Marrou in the first instance argued that Augustine was a poor writer,[19] the general feeling today is that he was an extremely talented one. Someone who, not unlike the famous autobiographers who came after him such as Goethe, Joyce and Proust, unravelled the inner reality of his personality thanks to language. It was language that shaped his inner life, and language was not the reflection of his being but rather what shaped his being, in the same sense as he believed the Word shaped the world.

But let's face it. This effect of language, characterized by its multiplicity and making it impossible to speak in a meaningful way about God, is also present in the Trinity itself once we introduce the Word of God. Of course, human language loses its sense when it can no longer distinguish between love, beauty, mercy and so on, but the same goes also for the divine Word. If this Word has to reflect all the qualities of the godhead, then it will fail to be language anymore. No two-nature doctrine is possible. It is not

---

[18] A very fine analysis of the Augustinian language and its consequences was written by Philip G. Porter, 'Inheriting Wittgenstein's Augustine: A Grammatical Investigation of the Incarnation', *New Blackfriars* 100(2019) 452–73, who criticizes Augustine's concept of the Incarnation and concludes that all this is due to the inadequacy that results from the Fall. That is exactly the other way round. There is no real inadequacy unless it is related to the divine that has another kind of infinity than language.
[19] An opinion he revoked in the later editions of his famous work, H-I. Marrou, *Saint Augustin et la fin de la culture antique*, Paris 1949/1986, *Retractatio*, 623–702.

possible to argue, on the one hand, that human language cannot conceive of the divine reality while maintaining, on the other hand, that there is a divine Word also characterized by an infinite multiplicity but that nevertheless reflects perfectly God's being, as well as His simplicity. That is simply overcharging the possibilities of language. In that case, there is only the Plotinian solution of suggesting that the divine Word must be situated beyond language, similar to the way the One is beyond being. If the divine Word is really a word, part of language, it cannot surpass the dichotomy of *similis/dissimilis*. The divine Word, however, is perfect beauty, grace, love and so on. It does not know any dissimilarity. In fact, its meaning is endless, yet without meaning. In a way this is a tragic development. At the very moment God reaches out for man, He does so by His Word but, at that particular moment, the divine simplicity cannot be conceived of as anything other than falling into pieces. This is something that cannot be avoided by a simple appeal to the doctrine of the two natures of Christ. Indeed, the only solution would have been to adopt the Plotinian way out – the way of emanations. There is indeed, says Plotinus, a divine simplicity: there is the One, but we cannot relate Him to our ordinary reality because it must be beyond being. Yet it pours itself out in forms of reality that still resemble the One but that nevertheless can be connected to language. Moreover, it is not a resemblance characterized by an absolute divide, such as Augustine was obliged to introduce because he had to respect the absolute difference between the Creator and the creation.

Echo revisited

Thus, regarding the question of whether Augustine held a theology that was part of the incarnation, the answer must be negative. Admittedly, language reflected in a certain way the divine reality, but it was unable to do so in an acceptable way. It was too colourful, too rich, too manifold. Now, it is precisely due to that endless variety that it necessarily betrays the One who created it. Undoubtedly, one might argue that there exist some exceptions. For instance, is it not true that language used in a confession, in prayer, in thanksgiving, is a univocal and true language? Indeed, the words used in these moments can be considered true. However, their truth does not concern the divine reality; there is no reflection of divine truth, but on the contrary, they concern the human one. Compared to the reality of what we want to express by these words, we remain stumbling, speaking in fits and starts. So, to be honest, our words are only fragments of what should be said; they are attempts, trying to fill themselves with a reality they cannot attain. Then, is there any other conclusion possible than that Augustine pictured the wounded language of Echo? Echo, in love with the One who constantly flew from her, was left with words she could only shout, but which lacked real power. They floated in the air, focusing on the One they wanted to honour with their infinite variety, but they were refused. Language, in Augustine's view, is a love story without a happy ending. It is a tragic story, just as Echo's love story is. In the end, though theological language could have been part of the incarnation, this love story ends with a reality that contains increasingly less reality. It gradually loses its character of reflecting the Incarnation that is represented by the divine Word and no longer has a 'bodily' structure, so to speak. It loses itself in an infinite multiplicity, according to Augustine's famous words: *unum a quo in multa defluximus*, the One from whom we are poured out in multiplicity.[20] But was Echo to blame? Had she done anything wrong by falling in love with Narcissus? Ovid nowhere suggests she had. The only thing one might conclude from the myth is that love is something where the lovers essentially act on an equal footing. The lover is not greater, more important, than the beloved, nor is it the other way round. That is indeed what Augustine plainly admits in his trinitarian doctrine: between the Father, the Son and the Spirit, there is an absolute equality.[21] However, this equality cannot be applied to the relationship between man and God because the latter created the first. If, however, such is the case, then the question arises: is love conceivable without this fundamental equality? Is it right to speak of humans loving God but at the same time being inferior to Him? Or is this the final trap language has prepared: love

---

[20] *Conf.* X,29,40.
[21] Cp. Mary Clark, 'De Trinitate', in, Èleonore Stump, ed., *The Cambridge Companion to Augustine*, Cambridge 2001, 91–102.

betrayed by language? This would mean that even the notion of inferiority is poorly chosen. In reality it all boils down to language betraying being and being betraying language. Love exists, of course, but once we start to speak about it, we betray it. That is the tragic of Echo: it is not even her love that fails to touch the heart of stone of Narcissus, it is her language that betrays her feelings. This means language does not betray her love because she speaks of it and expresses it, unveiling something that hitherto was hidden and secret; no, it betrays love because it reveals the unbridgeable gap between language and reality. Hence, it can only produce fear, the fear that frightened Narcissus and that he could only calm by looking at a perfect image, which could not be affected even by language. The following might be considered the hidden question of this famous myth: is love always producing betrayal? For that is now the conclusion: language betraying reality. In Augustine's view there is one exception, however: the divine Word that does not betray the ultimate reality but reflects it perfectly. However, this Word seems to betray words as it does not share the division and multiplicity that language brings about. Apparently, there are two kinds of lovers, both longing for each other, but unable to overcome the betrayal that language brings about. What we are witnessing is a love story, a love story between God and man, between Narcissus and Echo, in which language undermines each possible love. It is multiplicity against simplicity and apparently there are no means to overcome this opposition, even if only for a moment. Hence, theology does not belong to the incarnation and Augustine creates a new version of the story of Echo. That may be an amazing conclusion for someone who loved language as much as Augustine did. However, it also explains that, in the end, there was no other solution than to invoke the divine grace in order to restore a reality that at each moment was betrayed. In Augustine's view, the divine Word is the only means capable of restoring the shortcomings of human language. He overlooked, however, the fact that this divine Word could not really adopt a two-nature model, for it would fall back into the antinomy of similar/dissimilar. Moreover, as we are dealing with a love story, this grace can only be bestowed by an arbitrary choice. Once again, the divine embrace of language is a kiss of death to language. This is where it all ends up in Augustine's later works.

Conclusion

The question we wanted to answer was whether we could understand more of Augustine's concept of image. The notion proved to be a complicated one. Since Plato, it had a double nature. Not only did it reflect the original, but it also revealed a dissimilarity that was difficult to understand. Apparently, a kind of dissimilarity was unavoidable, but without there being a reason for this insufficiency. That was not only a kind of conundrum; it also had moral implications. Men was not able, in the view of Plato and afterwards that of Augustine, to avoid being caught up in a kind of darkness. This darkness could be pictured as a cave in which people were held in custody, unable to free themselves and to see the truth. Obviously, this was still a mere epistemological picture, at least in first instance. However, at a later stage it also became a moral picture; that was once we had concluded that human beings themselves could be considered the ultimate shadows, representing the inability to achieve and to attain the good. Next, Augustine created a similar universe in which human beings indeed were the ultimate shadows. This time, the prison was not a cave; it was the sinful state in which people have lived since the Fall. There is no way of escaping this prison unless God's grace delivers us from this evil state of being. Yet this fallen state is visible in the incapacity to see the truth. Therefore, the Augustinian picture is at the start a moral one (sin), producing an epistemological divide between the divine and the human. Indeed, Augustine reverses the roles of ontology and morals. Plato started with ontology, and Augustine switches to the moral ground and deduces from the moral deficiency an epistemological gap, thus revealing a split in the reality. Hence, this dissimilarity exists between humans and God, both in a moral and ontological sense, that can only be explained by sin. This sin, then, has to be an original one. However, an analysis of this original sin only reveals it to be the *causa formalis* of the need to preserve God's goodness. Indeed, the platonic solution of a Demiurge, looking at the Good without being identical with it, was not acceptable to Augustine. Original sin is therefore not about sin but about the need to find a solution for the inexplicable presence of evil in the creation. It is about the absolute requirement to never blame God for the presence of evil. Yet it does not explain how humans 'invented' evil, where the shadow came from and how it installed itself in the creation. Once again, sin tries to explain the origin of the shadow but fails to do so as it does not explain the nature of human beings, only the trespassing of God's commandments. Why this happened, however, remains an open question.

That was where Augustine's invention of similarity/dissimilarity entered the scene. Dissimilarity became the keyword in the relationship between God and humans both in a moral and ontological sense. Dissimilarity was therefore also the decisive characteristic of the relationship between the image and its original. This implies that the referential nature of an image is a broken one. There is a story behind the image, but we can only hear some scattered fragments of it. Therefore, it is dissimilarity, both epistemologically and morally, that produces the prison of ignorance and moral failure in which humans find themselves again. There is no possibility of reconstructing the story; there is only a deconstruction that is a definite one. The sole possibility to escape from this deconstruction is through a completely new creation, a recreation. But, even then, dissimilarity will remain. A complete identification with the divine, a real deification, is impossible. Yet there is also the other side of the coin. The image, by nature, can do nothing other than resemble the original. It refers to the original and this reference is not a neutral state of being, but an active process of longing and thriving. It is driven by the desire for unification. There is a deep longing for the original that, unfortunately, can never be satisfied. The image is part of the deconstruction while still longing for the construction and reconstruction. It is deeply characterized by its double and paradoxical nature: it strives towards the divine as a most constructive move, but at the same time it is doomed to fail, without this failure being explicable. There is similarity but the dissimilarity prevails. In fact, this whole dynamic pervading the image, its deep longing for the original, is nothing less than a love story.

The next stage then is to admit that this love story is a complicated one. It is not only about the image longing for the original, but also about language longing for being. Yet it is here that matters become not only complicated but also tragic, for it is not merely a case of language not being able to reveal the fullness of being – it is no less a matter of betrayal. It is betrayal because language knows of its own infinity, it knows of its own need to split an unbroken reality into many parts. It thus knows it betrays the reality it wants to picture. It is not merely a matter of an image incapable of reflecting the original – it is a matter of betrayal. Language and its infinity are the counterpart of God's infinity. Yet they are each other's opposite. There is the infinity of the One that knows of no internal differences, and there is the infinity of language producing precisely the infinite possibilities of differentiation. This, finally, is the merger of similarity and dissimilarity. The shadow we looked for is language that loves being but that betrays it at the same time. There is indeed a shadow: divine infinity has a shadow called language. This shadow cannot do anything else other than imagine the divine reality, but at the same time it betrays this latter reality. The image is always a variety, one of the many possibilities that reflection offers. Precisely, the image speaks a language that tries to create a place where the ultimate being can dwell, for that is its most important longing: to create a place where it could treasure the divine reality. Yet at the same time it knows this is not possible, for the language the image speaks is the very opposite of being: it bears an infinity in itself that is the opposite of the infinity of the divine being. It is this contradiction that creates, at the end, the moral vacuum that the shadow took as its shelter. The paradoxical effect, however, is that the story of this divine being must be told, it must be voiced. Language must play its role with regard to being but it is not capable of doing so in a constructive manner. Sure, there is an original story, an original love which celebrates an inconceivable unification, but that story, though it must be told, cannot be told. There is a script but in the end the protagonists are actors in a play without a script. They are the echoes of Echo.

One of the first to fully understand the implications of this paradoxical theology was of course Julian of Aeclanum. Sure, his ideal joins the old ideals of a life of virtue and even of asceticism. They were ideals that partly belonged to the sphere of classical philosophy, partly to that of early Christianity. However, he recognized that the real issue at stake was neither the opposition between merits and grace, nor the one between free will and predestination. No, he realized that Augustine was tearing apart the story of the Incarnation, of a Word spreading itself into an infinity of words and languages. He defended, so to speak, the integrity of the story, its Pentecostal dimension, and opposed himself to the deconstructive tendencies he discovered in Augustine's theology. When he reproached Augustine to introduce a theology based on Fate,[22] he was exactly pointing at this deconstructive approach, which he considered to no longer be a Christian one. He pointed at the moral vacuum, dubbed Fate, that Augustine had created. Pelagianism, however, was rejected and the Augustinian approach of the divine became the yardstick of what a correct theology was. It remained so even after the Reformation, and both Catholics and Protestants based their essential views on the relationship between God and men on the theology of the bishop of Hippo. However, both traditions harboured the illusion that it was still possible to discover the original story hidden behind the fragments of history. In the case of Protestantism, iconoclasm can be considered a final attempt to discover a one-dimensional space behind the multilayered language of images. The devastating storm of deconstructing any language based on physical images took the dissimilarity between the highest being and the images that were to tell its story seriously, and it wanted to safeguard the uniqueness of this being. At least, that is the most positive approach one can suggest when it comes to this highly destructive event. Taken as such, iconoclasm, reinforced by a theology of *sola fide* already proposed by Ockham, was an attempt to prove that the divine was still accessible. How? By presupposing that it could be found in the Bible that had long been identified with the sole Word identical to the divine being itself. It was the idea that humans could undo themselves from their inborn multiplicity and become like an empty church where the Bible has the exclusive right to fill this blank space. But, of course, in reality there was no empty space, and the idea that only the Bible had the right to speak overlooked the fact that even those words cannot be heard without taking into account their context. A lecture *a prima facie*, pretending this is the truth, is not possible. Words, even those of the Bible, can never be taken at face value. Nevertheless, Protestants continued to believe in this *sola scriptura*; they continued to stick to the idea of a *solus* (*sola fide, sola gratia, sola scriptura*) – meaning a kind of divine simplicity – believing there still was an empty room where

---

[22] Cf. C. *Duas Ep. Pel.* II,5,10: *Unde autem hoc eis uisum fuerit nobis obicere quod fatum asseramus sub nomine gratiae.* Compare also II,6,12 where Augustine expands on the theme of grace considered as Fate.

only the Bible dares to speak, where the grace of God is nothing less than His purest revelation and where belief is a direct contact with the divine. This was a development that in itself already qualified every word and every language outside the Bible as dissimilarity. Moreover, the participation model Augustine had still half-heartedly proposed as a possibility to overcome the dissimilarity also proved unacceptable to Protestant eyes. However, the model survived in the Catholic tradition, albeit in a moderate form. Nevertheless, in the end the Roman Catholic Church held a conviction similar to the Protestant one. For, in the Catholic view, there also existed the suggestion of the possibility of an unbroken story, as well as the ability to have access to this story, to the divine. Only this time it was not the Bible that could guarantee such look to the divine: it was the Church. Both traditions, however, considered sin as the cave in which humans were the inmates. Unfortunately, therefore, neither Catholics nor Protestants dared to think about the equivalence between the infinity of language and the infinity belonging to the divine One. Humans, though images of God, remained cripples and the ensuing Enlightenment, with its optimistic, rationalist and anti-religious mentality, was an almost foreseeable reaction.

Meanwhile, rationalism in the sense of the Enlightenment did not bring us an answer to the questions raised. On the contrary, it complicated matters in an unexpected way. The positive aspect was that the Enlightenment explored the endless possibilities of language and of images. It discovered, thanks to its emphasis on Reason, new territories of knowledge; it valued individual freedom very much; and in that sense it fully concentrated on the infinity that belonged to the world of humans. The less positive aspect was that it often put aside the infinity belonging to the One. This is not to say the Enlightenment in itself was anti-religious, but it strongly opposed the traditional structures of Church and belief, as well as the relationship between Church and the State. Belief, contrary to the Ancien Régime, had become an individual conviction, rather incomparable to the general perspective that was crafted by Reason and rationality. Humans as an image of the divine were no longer a common ground. On the contrary, it became a story that was a private one. Humans were individuals and what they shared was their rationality. Reason and rationality became the parameters of human existence, implying that morality was also to be found within the realm of rationality. Indeed, the Enlightenment taught that rationality and knowledge would contribute to solving the moral problems people met in their lives. Knowledge would show us the way out of the cave of ignorance and irrationality. It would reveal a universal moral law with its solid criteria for good and evil (Kant). That was perhaps the most deceitful idea of the eighteenth and nineteenth centuries. Rationality and morality proved not to be coherent and complementary; on the contrary, rationality could very well be the instrument of irrationality, and both could team up. Indeed, after the twentieth century, any optimism that rationality would lead to a morally more responsible humanity had been swept away. Hence, morality has once again become one of the most pressing issues our era has to deal with, and the same goes for the question regarding the image we have created of a human being.

Who are we, what are we and what is the story we are telling? Is there still any story to tell or can we only repeat the words of ancient narratives we still bear in mind, but in a fragmented and distorted way? It is probably the latter version. Modern narratives are often distorted stories, composed of a mixture of ideals (often secularized Christian ideals) and well understood self-interest. The main question to be answered then concerns the notion of a human being as an image – either an image of the divine or an image without any underlying narrative. To be honest, what we have discovered in this study is that such a clear-cut alternative has never existed. From the outset, the notion of image as framed by Augustine was a distorted one. It was both humans being the image of God, as well as human beings attracted by other realities than the divine one, and becoming beings without an underlying narrative. The mould cast by Augustine proved to be a solid one, capable of surviving secularism. It easily survived even without the background of Christian belief. What was this mould? Essentially it was the notion of an image qualified by its dissimilarity to the highest being. The highest being became unknowable and therefore its existence no longer mattered. This Augustinian mould was not even broken by the Enlightenment, which in fact replaced the highest being by Reason. However, Reason proved to be as inaccessible as God, and it often covered up strange forms of irrationality – as Freud clearly showed in his works. Once again dissimilarity showed itself to be more powerful than we had expected. Man was not the perfect image of Reason; he was sometimes reasonable and sometimes reasonably irrational. The conclusion, then, must be that the Augustinian heritage has had not only a longstanding influence on the history of mentality, but it has also proved to be an impediment to thinking in other terms about the image humans represent. What we actually witness, therefore, is the Christian story behind our world of images increasingly crumbling. Yet this is not only due to external factors but also to the unclear and twisted message Christianity told about the image of the divine that humans could represent. Hence, it did not take long to meet images in our times that were completely satisfied with being a mere image without any story. Images that apparently were aware of the fact that we were already reduced to the state of Echo, and who used this void to be able to echo the void others felt but weren't aware of. That, finally, allowed them to manipulate the masses and to suggest they would fill this inner void. It is complete deconstruction pretending to be construction.

If this is the outcome, where did Augustine hesitate to take further steps? The answer is exactly in the domain of morality. The decision he made was to refuse to compare the divine infinity with the infinity belonging to language. This meant that the referential quality of language became flawed. Hence, being and language became separated, which created in fact a double ontology instead of an ontology dealing with one, undivided yet multilayered, reality to which language refers. Indeed, he refused to trace the trail Plotinus had already made, which, incidentally, is not always an approach without danger of simplification. Many have thought of human beings as reflecting the divine infinity, sometimes suggesting there was a kind of divine spark, sometimes believing one could raise himself to the level of divinity, such as by being ordained. However, such a solution does not solve the moral problem. On the contrary, it often disguises the problem. Suffice it to think of the case of sexual abuse, where the claim to be part of the divinity led to a behaviour in which the 'divine' was only a shield to hide abuse. Therefore, the idea of language reflecting the divine being can easily be misused, simplified and then become a blind alley. What, by contrast, might have been a fruitful starting point is to start with the conclusion that language has lost its particular qualities when it comes to the divine being. Is it not true that in God there is no difference between His wisdom, His greatness, His mercy, His justice and so on? This means that these words lose their sense (unless this wisdom, greatness and so on are nothing other than the perfection of human models of wisdom, greatness and so on). This goes in particular for the notion of the Good. The definition Augustine applies is that something is good because God considers it good. God does not consider things good because they are good; they are good because He is their origin, even if we would consider it bad or evil. Now, if the notion of Good has no sense anymore within the realm of the divine being, the only solution then will be to argue that no real relationship exists between God and Good. What is good is not good because God calls it good (the notion would then lose its sense); it is good because humans call it good. Consequently, morality belongs entirely to the realm of human beings. Of course, that was not the way Augustine wanted to choose. He preferred to call God the ultimate good, without us knowing what this ultimate good could be. For instance, we are no longer capable of understanding God's justice when it comes to notions as merit, grace and predestination.

Now, this being said, and having concluded that morality belongs exclusively to the realm of human beings, we should not underestimate to what extent Augustine was right regarding the moral capacities of human beings. He was right in arguing that humans are not capable of realizing what they consider to be the good. There is, apparently, something of a perspective we cannot yet grasp. Yet, this inability cannot be called a shortcoming as if there were a kind of perfect good which humans cannot realize. To be honest: there is no perfect good. Good is only what is good in a certain situation at a certain time for certain people. Morality cannot deal with the idea of an absolute or perfect good, because this denies the fact that the good is tied to a certain time, to certain conditions. That is what morality often reduces to a kind of umbrella we take with us when the sun is shining but that does not protect us when heavy rains are falling. Morality, alas, is often fighting the last war, trying to apply lessons that were valuable during said war but which have lost their worth in current times. Hence, a perfect or absolute good cannot be conceived. This is what language shows us: there is always a range of many choices and options that necessarily break down the notion of one unbroken reality, of a unique story that covers the many aspects of our life. So indeed, taking our starting point in the Good, it will be difficult to follow Augustine, precisely because it is one of the elements causing the dissimilarity of the image and the distorted history of human nature that was its consequence.

However, Augustine had also this other starting point, – namely love. His story was meant to be a love story, although he believed that this love was also a kind of betrayal. Yet, his idea that love had a trinitarian structure (the lover, the beloved and love itself), uniting what was divided, was a brilliant approach. It does not deal with a perfect or absolute love, but rather deals with the differences in our lives without calling them dissimilarities. The language of love cannot be reduced to one simple word: it needs an infinite vocabulary. This is a vocabulary that can join God's infinity without taking away the difference between the human and the divine, but it no longer needs the notion of sin. What he could not achieve in the domain of morality, an ever changing good, he did achieve in his concept of love. Love as a dynamic that constantly unfolds itself in different forms, in different colours, but that cannot be reduced to a solid structure in which God's immobility is the starting point. On the contrary, what Augustine tries to picture is a love that depends on the words we choose, on the image we create.

BIBLIOGRAPHY

Alfaric, Prosper, *L'évolution intellectuelle de saint Augustin*, Paris 1918.
Anderson, Gary A., *Sin: A History*, Yale 2009.
Anderson, L., *Autobiography*, London 2001.
Arendt, Hanna, *Eichmann in Jerusalem: A Report on the Banality of Evil*, London 1963.
Armstrong, A. H., *Saint Augustine and Christian Platonism*, Villanova 1967.
Armstrong, A. H., together with Markus, R. A., *Christian Faith and Greek Philosophy*, London 1964.
Ayres, Lewis, *The Christological Context of Augustine's De Trinitate XIII: Towards Relocating Books VIII–XV*, Augustinian Studies 29(1998), 111–39.
Ayres, Lewis, 'The Fundamental Grammar of Augustine's Trinitarian Theology', in, Robert Dodaro, George Lawless, eds., *Augustine and His Critics*, New York 2000, 51–76.
Ayres, Lewis, '"Remember That You Are Catholic" (serm. 52.2): Augustine on the Unity of the Triune God', *Journal of Early Christian Studies* 8(2000) 39–82.
Ayres, Lewis, *Nicaea and Its Legacy: An Approach to Fourth-Century Trinitarian Theology*, Oxford 2004.
Ayres, Lewis, *Augustine and the Trinity*, Cambridge 2010.
Bateman, John A., *Text and Image, a Critical Introduction to the Visual-Verbal Divide*, London 2014.
Van Bavel, Tarcisius J., *Recherches sur la christologie de saint Augustin. L'humain et le divin dans le Christ d'après saint Augustin*, Fribourg 1954.
Bermon, Emmanuel, *Le Cogito dans la pensée de Saint Augustin*, Paris 2001.
Bobonich, Chris, 'Plato on Akrasia and Knowing Your Own Mind', in, Christopher Bobonich and Pierre Destrée, eds., *Akrasia in Greek Philosophy: From Socrates to Plotinus*, Leiden/Boston 2007, 41–60.
Bochet, Isabelle, *Saint Augustin et le désir de Dieu*, Paris 1982.
Bochet, Isabelle, *Le statut de l'image dans la pensée augustinienne*, Archives de Philosophie 72(2009), 249–69.

Boagaert, Sophie, Kern, Etienne, and Kern-Boquel, Anne, *Les énigmes du moi. Saint Augustin. Les Confessions (livre X), Musset, Lorenzaccio, Leiris, L'Âge d'homme*, Paris 2008.

Bonner, Gerald, *Freedom and Necessity: St Augustine's Teaching on Divine Power and Human Freedom*, Washington 2007.

Bouton-Touboulic, Anne-Isabelle, 'Qu'il n'y a pas d'amour sans connaissance: étude d'un argument du De Trinitate, livres VIII–XV', in Emmanuel Bermon and Gerald O'Daly, eds., *Le De Trinitate de Saint Augustin, Exégèse, logique et noétique*, Paris 2012, 181–203.

Boyer, Frédéric, *Saint Augustin, Les Aveux*, Paris 2008.

Brachtendorf, Johannes, *Die Struktur des Menslichen Geistes nach Augustinus. Selbstreflexion und Erkenntnis Gottes in De Trinitate*, Tübingen 1998.

Brachtendorf, Johannes, *The Goodness of Creation and the Reality of Evil: Suffering as a Problem in Augustine's Theodicy*, Augustinian Studies 31(2000), 79–92.

Brachtendorf, Johannes, *Gott und Sein Bild – Augustinus' De Trinitate im Spiegel gegenwärtiger Forschung*, Paderborn 2000.

Brisson, Luc, *The Reception of the Parmenides before Proclus*, Zeitschrift für Antikes Christentum 12(2008), 99–113.

Brisson, Luc, 'Reminiscence in Plato', in, John Dillon, Marie-Elise Zovko, eds., *Platonism and Forms of Intelligence*, Berlin 2008, 179–90.

Brockmeier, I. and Carbaugh, D., *Narrative and Identity: Studies in Autobiography, Self and Culture*, Amsterdam 2001.

Peter Brown, *Augustine of Hippo: A Biography, new edition*, London 2000.

Brown, P., *The Body and Society: Men, Women, and Sexual Renunciation in Early Christianity*, New York 1988.

Burke, Peter, *The Fabrication of Louis XIV*, New Haven 1992.

Burrus, Virginia, Jordan, Mark D., and Mackendrick, Karmen, *Seducing Augustine: Bodies, Desires, Confessions*, New York 2010.

Burton, Philip, *Language in the Confessions of Augustine*, Oxford 2007.

Carey, Philip, *Augustine's Invention of the Inner Self: The Legacy of a Christian Platonist*, Oxford 2003.

Carey, Philip, *Outward Signs: The Powerlessness of External Things in Augustine's Thought*, Oxford/New York 2008.

Castro, Andrés Fabián Henao, 'Slavery in Plato's Allegory of the Cave: Badiou, Alain, Rancière, Jacques, and the Militant Intellectual from the Global South', *Theatre Survey* 58(2017), 86–107.

Clark, Mary, 'De Trinitate', in Èleonore Stump ed., *The Cambridge Companion to Augustine*, Cambridge 2001, 91–102.

Clausen, Ian, *On Love, Confession, Surrender and the Moral Self*, New York 2018.

Cloete, Michael, 'Revisiting Plato's Republic: Towards a Praxis of Justice', *Phronimon* 11(2010), 65–79.
Collobert, Catherine, 'The Platonic Art of Myth-Making: Myth as Informative Phantasma', in Catherine Collobert, Pierre Destrée, Francisco J. Gonzalez, eds., *Plato and Myth: Studies on the Use and Status of Platonic Myths*, Leiden/Boston 2012, 87–108.
Cooper, John M., 'Plato and Aristotle on "Finality" and (Self-)Sufficiency', in John M. Cooper, ed., *Knowledge, Nature and the Good, Essays on Ancient Philosophy*, Princeton 2004, 270–308.
Courcelle, Pierre, *Recherches sur les Confessions de saint Augustin*, Paris 1950.
Cristini, Carlo and Ploton, Louis, *Mémoire et autobiographie*, Gerontologie et société 32(2009), 75–95.
Crouse, Robert, 'Paucis mutatis verbis: St Augustine's Platonism', in Robert Dodaro and George Lawless, eds., *Augustine and His Critics*, New York 2000, 37–50.
Davidson, Donald, 'Plato's Philosopher', in Terence Irwin and Martha C. Nussbaum, eds., *Virtue, Love & Form: Essays in Memory of Gregory Vlastos*, Edmonton, Alberda 1993, 179–94.
Dodaro, Robert and Lawless, George, eds., *Augustine and His Critics: Essays in Honour of Gerald Bonner*, London/New York 2000.
James J. O'Donnell, *Augustine: A New Biography*, New York 2005.
Drever, Matthew, *Image, Identity and the Forming of the Augustinian Soul*, Oxford 2013.
Eakin, P. J., *Living Autobiographically: How We Can Create Identity in Narrative*, Ithaca 2008.
Edwards, Mark, *Catholicity and Heresy in the Early Church*, London 2009.
Edwards, Mark, *Image, Word and God in the Early Christian Centuries*, London 2013.
Enos, Richard Leo, Thompson, Roger et al., *The Rhetoric of St. Augustine of Hippo: De Doctrine Christiana & the Search for a Distinctly Christian Rhetoric*, Waco Texas 2008.
Fattal, Michel, *Plotin chez Augustin. Suivi de Plotin face aux Gnostiques*, Paris 2006.
Fejfer, Jane, 'Selves and Others: Ways of Expressing Identity in the Roman Male Portrait', in Jane Fejfer ed., *Roman Portraits in Context*, Berlin/New York 2008, 262–327.
Flasch, Kurt, *Logik des Schreckens. Augustinus von Hippo: Die Gnadenlehre von 397*, Mainz 1990.
Folkenflik, R., ed., *The Culture of Autobiography: Constructions of Self-Representation*, Stanford 1993.
Folkmarson Käll, Lisa, 'A Voice of Her Own: Echo's Own Echo', *Continental Philosophy Review* 48(2015), 59–75.

Frede, Michael, *A Free Will: Origins of the Notion in Ancient Thought*, Berkeley 2011.
Freedberg, David, *The Power of Images: Studies in the History and Theory of Response*, Chicago/London 1989.
Gerson, Lloyd P., *Knowing Persons: A Study in Plato*, Oxford 2006.
Gildenhard, Ingo and Zissos, Andrew, 'Ovid's Narcissus (Met. 339–510): Echoes of Oedipus', *The American Journal of Philosophy* 121(2000), 129–47.
Gioia, Luigi, *The Theological Epistemology of Augustine's De Trinitate*, Oxford 2008.
Grabe, Maria Elizabeth, and Bucy, Erik P., *Image Bite Politics: News and the Visual Framing of Elections*, Oxford 2010.
Greenblatt, Stephen, *Renaissance Self-Fashioning: From More to Shakespeare*, Chicago 2005.
Greenblatt, Stephen and Gallagher, Catherine, *Practising New Historicism*, Chicago 2000.
Hadot, Pierre, *Porphyre et Victorinus*, Paris 1968.
Hadot, Pierre, *Etudes de Philosophie Ancienne*, Paris 1998.
Hall, James, *The Self-Portrait: A Cultural History*, London 2014.
Hanby, Michael, *Augustine and Modernity*, London 2003.
Harper, Kyle, *From Shame to Sin: The Christian Transformation of Sexual Morality in Late Antiquity*, Harvard 2013.
Harrison, Carol, *Augustine: Christian Truth and Fractured Humanity*, Oxford 2000.
Harrison, Carol, *Rethinking Augustine's Early Theology: An Argument for Continuity*, Oxford 2006.
Harrison, Carol, *The Art of Listening in the Early Church*, Oxford 2013.
Harte, Verity and Lane, Melissa, eds., *Politeia in Greek and Roman Philosophy*, Princeton 2013, 139–54.
Hawrad, Joseph, *The Ghost of Perfection: Searching for Humanity*, Eugene Oregon 2017.
Heidegger, M., *Being and Truth*, Bloomington 2010. Translation of the original *Sein und Wahrheit*.
Hocks, Mary E. and Kendrick, Michelle R., eds., *Eloquent Images: Words and Images in the Age of New Media*, Cambridge, MA 2003.
Hollingworth, Miles, 'Closer to Augustine: Speculating on the Recent Past, and Future, of Augustine Scholarship', *The Expository Times* 125(2013), 220–9.
Hollingworth, Miles, *Saint Augustine of Hippo: An Intellectual Biography*, London 2013.
Hollingworth, Miles, *Ludwig Wittgenstein*, Oxford 2018.

Hollingworth, Miles, 'Augustine and the Codes of Life', in Barry David, ed., *Passionate Mind: Essays in Honor of John M. Rist*, Academia Verlag 2019, 393–414.

Horowitz, J. Gordon, *Gettostadt: Lodz and the Making of a Nazi City*, Harvard 2009.

Jin, Seunga Venus and Ryu, Ehri, '"The Paradox of Narcissus and Echo in the Instagram Pond" in Light of the Selfie Culture from Freudian Evolutionary Psychology: Self-Loving and Confident but Lonely', *Journal of Broadcasting & Electronic Media* 62(2018), 554–77.

Kahle, Lynn R. and Kim, Chung-Hyun, eds., *Creating Images and the Psychology of Marketing Communication*, London 2006.

Kany, Roland, *Augustins Trinitätsdenken*, Tübingen 2007.

Kurihara, Yuji, 'Plato on the Ideal of Justice and Human Happiness: Return to the Cave (Republic 519e–521b)', in Georgios Anagnostopoulos, ed., *Socratic, Platonic and Aristotelian Studies: Essays in Honour of Gerasimos Santos*, London/New York 2011, 271–9.

Lagouanère, Jérôme, *Intériorité et réflexivité dans la pensée de Saint Augustin: Formes et genèse d'une conceptualisation*, Paris 2012.

Lane Fox, Robin, *Augustine: Conversions to Confessions*, New York/London 2015.

Lancel, Serge, *Saint Augustin*, Paris 1999.

Lieu, Judith, *Christian Identity in the Jewish and Graeco-Roman World*, Oxford 2004.

Lieu, Judith, *Marcion and the Making of a Heretic: God and Scripture in the Second Century*, New York 2014.

Lyons, John D. Nichols Jr., Stephen G., eds., *Mimesis: From Mirror to Method, Augustine to Descartes*, Hanover/London 1982.

Madec, G., *Notes sur l'intelligence augustinienne de la foi*, REAug 17(1971)119–42.

Mann, William E., 'Augustine on Evil', in David Vincent Meconi, ed., *The Cambridge Companion to Augustine*, Cambridge 2014, 58–107.

Markschies, Christoph, *Gnosis und Christentum*, Berlin 2009.

Markus, R. A., '"Imago" and "Similitudo" in Augustine', *REAug* 10(1964), 125–43.

Markus, R. A., *Saeculum: History and Society in the Theology of St. Augustine*, Cambridge 1970/89.

Markus, R. A., *Christianity and the Secular*, Notre Dame 2006.

H-I. Marrou, *Saint Augustin et la fin de la culture antique*, Paris 1949/1986.

O'Meara, Dominic J., 'Explaining Evil in Late Antiquity', in Andrew P. Chignell, ed., *Evil: A History*, Oxford 2019, 130–154.

McGuirk, James N., 'Aletheia and Heidegger's Transitional Readings of Plato's Cave Allegory', *Journal of the British Society for Phenomenology* 39(2008), 167–85.

Meconi, David Vincent, 'Ravishing Ruin: Self-Loathing in Saint Augustine', *Augustinian Studies* 45(2014), 227–46.
Melot, Michel, 'L'image n'est plus ce qu'elle était', *Revue documentaliste Sciences de l'Information* 42(2005/6), 361–5.
Milano, Ronit, 'The Face of the Monarchy: Court Propaganda and the Portrait Bust', in Ronit Milano, *The Portrait Bust and French Cultural Politics in the Eighteenth Century*, Leiden/Boston 2015.
Morris, T. F., 'Plato's Cave', *South African Journal of Philosophy* 28(2009), 415–32.
Nightingale, Andrea, *Once out of Nature: Augustine on Time and the Body*, Chicago 2011.
Nussbaum, Martha, *The Fragility of Goodness: Luck and Ethics in Greek Tragedy and Philosophy*, Cambridge 2001.
Paulson, Ronald, *Sin and Evil: Moral Values in Literature*, Yale 2007.
Payne, Andrew, *The Teleology of Action in Plato's Republic*, Oxford 2017.
Politis, Vasili, 'The *Aporia* in the *Charmides* about Reflexive Knowledge and the Contribution to Its Solution in the Sun Analogy of the *Republic*', in Douglas Cairns, Fritz-Gregor Hermann and Terrence Penner, eds., *Pursuing the Good: Ethics and Metaphysics in Plato's Republic*, Edinburgh 2012, 231–50.
Porter, Philip G., 'Inheriting Wittgenstein's Augustine: A Grammatical Investigation of the Incarnation', *New Blackfriars* 100(2019), 452–73.
Pranger, B., 'Augustine and the Silence of the Sirens', *Journal of Religion* 91(2011), 64–77.
Queneau, Raymond, *Exercices de style*, Paris 1982.
Rappe, Sara, 'Self-knowledge and Subjectivity in the *Enneads*', in Lloyd P. Gerson, ed., *The Cambridge Companion to Plotinus*, Cambridge 1996, 250–74.
Rigby, Paul, 'Was Augustine a Narcissist?', *Augustinian Studies* 44(2013), 59–91.
Rist, John M., *Augustine: Ancient Thought Baptised*, Cambridge 1994.
Rist, John M., 'Democracy and Religious Values. Augustine on Locke, Lying and Individualism', St. Augustine Lecture 1997, *Augustinian Studies* 29(1998), 7–24.
Rist, J. M., Journal of Theological Studies 65(2014)309–12. Review of Jérôme Lagouanère, *Intériorité et réflexivité dans la pensée de Saint Augustin: Formes et genèse d'une conceptualisation*, Paris 2012.
Rombs, Ronnie J., *Saint Augustine and the Fall of the Soul: Beyond O'Connel and His Critics*, Catholic University of America Press 2006.
du Roy, Olivier, *L'intelligence de la foi en la Trinité selon saint Augustin*, Paris 1966.
Rowe, Christopher, 'The Form of the Good and the Good in Plato's Republic', in Douglas Kern, Fritz-Gregor Hermann and Terrence

Penner, eds., *Pursuing the Good. Ethics and Metaphysics in Plato's Republic*, Edinburgh 2012, 124–53.

Russell, Daniel C., 'Pleasure and Moral Psychology in Republic IV and IX', in Daniel C. Russell ed., *Plato on Pleasure and the Good Life*, Oxford 2005, 106–36.

Schmaus, M., *Die psychlogische Trinitätslehre des heiligen Augustinus*, Münster 1927.

Shuster, Marguerite, *The Fall and Sin: What We Have Become as Sinners*, Grand Rapids 2004.

Smalbrugge, Matthias, *Augustine's Reception of Augustine. And How to Write History, How to Compare Images*, Sacris Erudiri 58(2019)145–70.

Sourisse, Michel, 'Saint Augustin et le problème du mal: la polémique antimanichéenne', *L'esprit du temps* 19(2007), 109–14.

Stark, Judith Chelius, *Feminist Interpretations of Augustine*, Pennsylvania 2007.

Stock, Brian, *Augustine's Inner Dialogues: The Philosophical Soliloquy in Late Antiquity*, Cambridge 2010.

Stone, Greg, 'The Myth of Narcissus as a Surreptitious Allegory about Creativity', *Philosophy and Literature* 40(2016), 273–84.

Strózynski, Mateusz, 'There Is No Searching for the Self: Self-knowledge in Book X of Augustine's De Trinitate', *Phronesis* 58(2013), 280–300.

Szaif, Jan, 'Die Alêtheia in Platons Tugendlehre', in Marcel Van Ackeren, ed., *Platon verstehen. Themen und Perspektiven*, Darmstadt 2004, 183–209.

Taylor, Charles, *Sources of the Self: The Making of Modern Identity*, Harvard 1989.

Teske, R. J., 'The Image and Likeness of God in St. Augustine's *De Genesi ad Litteram Liber Imperfectus*', *Augustinianum* 30(1990), 441–51.

Turner, John, ed., *Plato's Parmenides and Its Heritage. Volume 1: History and Interpretation from the Old Academy to Later Platonism and Gnosticism*, Leiden/Boston 2010; Volume II, *Reception in Patristic, Gnostic and Christian Neoplatonic Texts*, Leiden/Boston 2010.

Vannier, Marie-Anne, *Saint Augustin*, Paris 2011.

Vinzent, Markus, *Writing the History of Early Christianity: From Reception to Retrospection*, Cambridge 2019.

Wetzel, James, 'Augustine on the Will', in Mark Vessey, ed., *A Companion to Augustine*, Oxford 2012, 339–52.

Wetering, Ernst Van De, ed., *A Corpus of Rembrandt Paintings: The Self-Portraits*, New York 2005.

Wilberding, James, 'Prisoners and Puppeteers in the Cave', *Oxford Studies in Ancient Philosophy* 27(2004), 117–39.

Williams, Rowan, *On Augustine*, London, New York 2016.

Wilson, Kenneth M., *Augustine's Conversion from Traditional Free Choice to 'Non-Free Will': A Comprehensive Methodology*, Tübingen 2018.

Wolf, Naomi, *The Beauty Myth: How Images of Beauty Are Used against Women*, New York 1990/2002.

Yin Yam, Cheuk and Dupont, Anthony, 'A Mind-Centered Approach of "Imago Dei": A Dynamic Construction in Augustine's *De Trinitate* XV', *Augustiniana* 62(2012), 7–43.

Young, Frances, 'Augustine's Hermeneutics and Postmodern Criticism', *A Journal of Bible and Theology* 58(2004), 42–55.

Young, Frances, *Biblical Exegesis and the Formation of Christian Culture*, Cambridge 1997.

Zovko, Marie-Elise, 'The Way Up and the Way Back Are the Same: Plato's Analogies of the Sun, the Line and the Cave and the Path Intelligence Takes', in John Dillon, Marie-Élise Zovko, eds., *Proceedings of the International Symposium Platonism and Forms of Intelligence*, Akademie Verlag, Berlin, 313–41.

Zwollo, Laela, *St. Augustine and Plotinus: The Human Mind as Image of the Divine*, Leiden/Boston 2018.

INDEX

Adam and Eve 68, 115. *See also* sin
akrasia (lack of self-knowledge) 31 n.12, 66
St Ambrose 40–1, 100
analogy 39, 90, 98, 98 n.3, 100
Arendt, Hannah, *Eichmann in Jerusalem: A Report on the Banality of Evil* 31 n.11
Aristotle, *Posterior Analytics* 51
atonement 68. *See also* sin
St Augustine 5, 20, 37–40, 42–4, 133. *See also* Plato
   absolute divide 73, 98, 126–7, 129, 138
   Ad Simplicianum 61
   ambivalence 48–9, 74–8, 116
   love and contempt 84–6
   memory 86–91
   biographies of 16 n.32
   causa deficiens 64 n.57, 80–1
   causa efficiens 64 n.57, 79–80
   Christianization of 99, 102
   Christology 41, 97, 99, 99 n.5
   Commentaries on Genesis 53
   Confessions 9 n.18, 14–18, 16 n.31, 38, 40–2, 59, 63, 64 n.56, 86–7, 89–90, 89 n.43, 98, 105, 114, 129 n.1, 136, 136 n.17
   Contra Duas Epistolas Pelagianorum 144 n.22
   De Civitate Dei 43–4, 69, 71, 78, 80–1, 81 n.28, 99

   De Diversis Quaestionibus 83 53
   De Doctrina Christiana 135, 135 f5
   De Genesi ad Litteram Imperfectus 55–6, 63–4, 70, 74, 81 n.28
   De Genesi contra Manichaeos 69
   De Libero Arbitrio 61 n.49, 62 n.52, 64 n.57
   De Vera Religione 44, 53–4
   free will 61 n.49, 62
   human will 59, 61–2, 61 n.49
   idea of sin (*see* sin)
   incarnation 38–9, 50, 57, 74, 133, 137 n.18, 138–40, 143
   moral vacuum 104, 129, 143–4
   participation 40, 76, 113, 129, 133, 145
   Reason 45, 49, 145–6
   similarity (image) 72, 113, 130, 138 (*see also* resemblance (*similitudo*))
      absolute 55–6
      and dissimilarity 39–40, 42, 44–51, 56–8, 60, 69, 73, 75–84, 86, 91, 110–11, 116, 132, 138, 141–3, 145
      and participation 51–3, 72–4, 76
   Soliloquies/Soliloquia 45, 51, 53, 56, 74–5

INDEX

theodicy 64 n.58, 79
trinitarian structure 96, 114–15, 139, 149
autobiography 14–18, 15 n.27, 20
aversio (turning away) 78–9, 81, 111–12. *See also conversio* (turning to/conversion)
Ayres, Lewis 40 n.3, 101, 101 n.22

beauty 27, 55, 78, 86, 110–11, 113, 138
and knowledge 11–12
senses of 59–60
The Bible 43, 99, 144–5
Boyer, Frédéric, *Saint Augustin, Les Aveux* 59 n.47
Bucy, Erik P., *Image Bite Politics: News and the Visual Framing of Elections* 19 n.34
Burke, Peter, *The Fabrication of Louis XIV* 2 n.2

Catholics 144–5
Christian/Christianity 15, 40–2, 53, 61, 63, 85, 99–103, 143–4, 146–7
sin (and salvation) 60, 62, 68 (*see also* sin)
Western 63
Christology 41, 97, 99, 99 n.5
Cloete, Michael, 'Revisiting Plato's Republic: Towards a Praxis of Justice' 33 n.16
construction/constructive approach 1–2, 13, 142–3, 147. *See also* destructive approach
conversio (turning to/conversion) 16, 16 n.31, 23, 26, 29, 78–9, 106, 111–12. *See also aversio* (turning away)

corporeal/corporeality 57, 70–1, 74, 104, 107–8, 110, 112–13, 115–18, 125
Courcelle, Pierre, *Recherches sur les Confessions de saint Augustin* 16 n.31
Covid-19 crisis 61
cupidity 81, 110–11

deconstruction/deconstructive approach 2, 142–4, 147
deification 63, 142
desire(s) 6–12, 14, 19–21, 25, 29, 35, 42, 49–50, 65–6, 77, 93–4, 112, 142
destructive approach 13. *See also* construction/constructive approach
De Trinitate 56, 74–6, 90, 93, 105 n.42, 109 n.50, 109 n.52, 112 nn.58–9, 116 nn.70–2, 118 n.74, 121 n.77, 123 n.79, 125 n.82, 129, 130 n.5, 131 n.8, 132 nn.9–11, 136
Augustinian *cogito* in 95, 109 n.50
double nature of images 112–16
general remarks on 94–104
love and knowledge 104–11, 131
self-reference/self-referential character 116–27
dissimilitudo/dissimilis (difference) 46, 53–4, 56, 75, 130, 132, 138
divine one 17, 75, 119, 132, 145–6
divine simplicity 132, 135, 138, 144
dreams 4, 9 n.18, 44, 46, 112

Dupont, Anthony, 'A Mind-
    Centered Approach of
    "Imago Dei": A Dynamic
    Construction in Augustine's
    De Trinitate XV', 91 n.46
du Roy, Olivier 90 n.45, 101 n.22,
    102

Echo and Narcissus 5–11, 8 n.14,
    82 n.33, 111, 119, 139–40,
    143, 147
    desire and fear 6–10, 12
    gender 7
    knowledge 10–11
    original and image 7–11, 9 n.19
    self identity/self-love 8–9
    selfies and myth of 6 n.10,
        11–13
emanations 63, 138
Enlightenment 21, 31, 145–6
epistemology/epistemological
    approach 16, 23, 30, 32, 50,
    52–5, 76–7, 91 n.46, 98, 98
    n.2, 107, 142
equality/inequality 56, 58, 73, 76,
    133–4, 139
evil 28, 30–1, 36, 63, 71, 76, 79
    n.24
    God and 79, 141
    good and 32 n.13, 36, 62–3,
    65, 79–80, 127, 146, 148
    (see also Good/Goodness)

Fate 32, 66, 144
Flasch, Kurt, *Logik des
    Schreckens. Augustinus von
    Hippo: Die Gnadenlehre
    von 397* 68 n.65
Freedberg, David, *The Power
    of Images: Studies in the
    History and Theory of
    Response* 2 n.1
French monarchy 2 n.2

Genesis 69–70, 72–4
Gerson, Lloyd P., *Knowing Persons:
    A Study in Plato* 25 n.5
Gioia, Luigi, *The Theological
    Epistemology of Augustine's
    De Trinitate* 98 n.2
Glaucon 21, 33
God 15, 17, 37, 51, 63, 108,
    126–7, 130, 133–4, 148–9
    The Creator/creation 51, 53,
    62–4, 70, 72–6, 79, 82–4,
    86–7, 97, 113, 116, 119,
    126, 129, 138
    divine law 67
    divine unity 56, 78, 132–3
    image of 37, 41–2, 58, 69–70,
    72–3, 73 n.17, 75, 82,
    84, 90, 104, 146 (see also
    image(s), divine)
    immaterial nature 41–3
    knowledge of 45–6, 51, 93–4,
    96, 108, 111
    love of 81–2, 93, 104, 125–6,
    132–3
    and man/human existence 39,
    42, 60, 75–6, 84, 86, 95, 97,
    113, 140, 142, 144
    and memory 86, 89–91
    Platonists idea of 43
    as similarity 53–8
    trinitarian structure of 56–8
    Word of God/divine Word
    74–5, 130–4, 137–9
godhead 56–8, 112, 125, 134, 137
Good/Goodness 24, 26–8, 30–1,
    34, 36, 42, 44, 62–4, 64
    n.56, 67, 78–80, 103–4,
    106, 111, 113, 127, 141,
    146, 148–9
    absolute/perfect 148
    and evil 32 n.13, 36, 62–3, 65,
    79–80, 127, 146, 148 (see
    also evil)

INDEX

ultimate 23, 27–8, 43, 53, 148
Grabe, Maria Elizabeth, *Image Bite Politics: News and the Visual Framing of Elections* 19 n.34
grace 59–60, 62, 65, 68, 77, 83–4, 97–8, 103–4, 126, 140–1, 143, 145
Greeks 2 n.2, 43, 66, 69
  hamartia (literature) 60, 63 n.54, 65, 67
  notion of failure 66
Greenblatt, Stephen
  Renaissance Self-Fashioning: From More to Shakespeare 3 n.3
  self-fashioning 3, 3 n.3, 14

hamartia (Greek literature) 60, 63 n.54, 65, 67
Harrison, Carol 40 n.3, 102
Harte, Verity 32 n.15
Heidegger, M., aletheia 35 n.20
Hollingworth, Miles 16 n.32, 99, 99 n.5, 103, 104 n.38
human/human beings 25–6, 28–9, 32 n.13, 35, 41–2, 57–62, 64–8, 75, 83, 98, 141–2, 146, 148
  and animals/animal instincts 70
  body and soul 42, 52, 70–1, 78, 87, 110, 113, 115, 118–19, 133
  divine *vs.* human words 74–5 (*see also* words/Word)
  fragility 30, 61–2, 64, 67
  and God 39, 42, 60, 75–6, 84, 86, 95, 97, 113, 140, 142, 144
  human existence 35, 39, 62, 69, 82–3, 145
  human mind (*see* mind (*animus*), human)
  human will 59, 61–2, 61 n.49
  imperfection 12, 59, 62–5
  language 134–8, 140 (*see also* language)
  moral failure 66, 78–84, 142
  nature of 57, 62, 66, 68, 72, 81, 83, 103, 142, 149
  sin/sinful nature (*see* sin)
  trinity and human dissimilarity 53–8

iconoclasm 144
identity 4, 7–9, 31, 40, 40 n.3, 101
image(s) 2–4, 20, 35–9, 82, 85, 87, 106, 108, 110–11, 125, 141, 147
  and autobiography 14–18, 15 n.27, 20
  cultural structures 4, 19
  divine 37, 41–4, 70, 73, 76, 82–3, 115, 117–19, 124–7, 130
  double nature of 20, 37, 112–16, 141
  Echo and Narcissus (*see* Echo and Narcissus)
  and emotions 2 n.1
  of God 37, 41–2, 58, 69–70, 72–3, 73 n.17, 75, 82, 84, 90, 104, 146
  ideal 5, 8, 10, 12, 25, 36, 113
  incarnational nature of 38–9, 50
  love and knowledge 107–11
  and memory 86, 91, 93–4, 98, 113–14
  multilayered 5, 12, 144
  new 3, 18
  ontological level 4–5, 13, 36
  and original 7–11, 9 n.19, 15, 17–20, 72–3, 83, 119, 142
  perfect 8, 14, 58, 73–4, 133, 136, 140

pure 113
and reality (*see* reality)
referential character of 16, 85
and selfies (*see* selfie)
and shadows 35–6
similarity (similitude) 72, 113, 130, 138
and dissimilarity of 39–40, 42, 44–51, 56–8, 60, 69, 73, 75–84, 86, 91, 110–11, 116, 132, 138, 141–3, 145
between God and man 71
and participation 51–3, 72–4, 76
imagine/imaginary/imagination 1–5, 13, 105, 113–15
imago/imago Dei 45 n.12, 91 n.46, 118
intellectus 96–7, 108, 124

Jane Fejfer, 'Selves and Others: Ways of Expressing Identity in the Roman Male Portrait' 2 n.2
Jews/Jewish 31 n.11, 42
Julian of Aeclanum 103, 143
justice 21–2, 24, 26–8, 30, 33–4, 33 n.16, 65, 71, 106–7, 147–8

Käll, Lisa Folkmarson, 'A Voice of Her Own: Echo's Own Echo' 9 n.19
knowledge 10, 11, 26, 32, 32 n.15, 46, 76, 93, 114, 120–1, 124–5, 130–1, 146
and beauty 11–12
of God 45–6, 51, 93–4, 96, 108, 111
love and 104–11
perfect 11, 14
prior 108–9
real 11, 25

self-knowledge 31 n.12, 108
and wisdom 23, 115

language 3, 37, 70, 74, 74 n.18, 106, 132–40, 142, 147. *See also* words/Word
and divine reality 37
and infinity 135–6, 142–3, 145, 147
multiplicity of 134–40, 144
One and the Many 133–4
love 94–6, 112–13, 120, 122–3, 140, 143, 149
and contempt 82 n.33, 84–6
Echo and Narcissus 6–12, 139–40
of God 81–2, 93, 104, 125–6, 132–3
and knowledge 104–11, 120
self-denying love 82
self-love 81–2, 124–5
and truth 89

Manichaeism/Manichaeans 41, 62, 69, 87
Good and Evil 32 n.13, 36, 41, 62–3, 79–80
Markus, R. A. 100, 103
'"Imago" and "similitudo" in Augustine' 45 n.12
Marrou, H-I. 137, 137 n.19
mathematics 46, 48, 51–2, 95
Meconi, David Vincent, 'Ravishing Ruin: Self-Loathing in Saint Augustine' 82 n.33
memory/memories 26–9, 44, 76, 86–91, 93, 105–6, 108–12, 109 n.52, 114–15, 125, 130, 135, 137
and image 86, 91, 93–4, 98, 113–14
and thinking 114 (*see also* thinking)

visible 12
and will 114
Milano, Ronit, 'The Face of the Monarchy: Court Propaganda and the Portrait Bust' 2 n.2
mimesis 5, 10, 24 n.3
mind (*animus*), human 26, 31 n.12, 52, 62, 70, 72, 73 n.14, 88, 90, 93, 95–7, 105–6, 108–13, 115–18, 120–2, 125, 129–31
morality 28, 103–4, 127, 145–9

narcissism/narcissistic 6 n.10, 9 n.18, 11, 13–14
Neoplatonism 63, 99–100
Neoplatonism/Neoplatonic/Neoplatonist model 40–1, 40 n.3, 63, 63 n.55, 78, 101
Nietzsche, Friedrich 18, 83
nothingness 48
Nussbaum, Martha 67

objects 9–11, 23–4, 26, 48, 61, 90, 93, 96, 106, 110, 115–16, 118, 122–4. See also subject
Oedipus, *Oedipus Rex* 66
ontology 5, 13, 26, 30, 36, 52, 54–5, 76, 97–8, 141, 147
optimism 32, 61–2, 146
Ovid 20, 139
  Metamorphoses 6, 61, 61 n.50 (*see also* Echo and Narcissus)

St Paul 71, 126
Pelagians/Pelagianism 59, 61–2, 65, 144
perfectionism 61, 65, 103
phantasma/phantasia 24, 24 n.3, 105
photoshopping 5, 12

Plato 5, 20–1, 24 n.3, 32 n.13, 37, 40–1, 43–4, 99, 136, 141.
  See also St Augustine
  akrasia (lack of self-knowledge) 31 n.12
  Allegory of the Cave 21
  good/ultimate good 23–4, 26–8, 30–2
  happiness 24
  human existence 35
  on human life 25–6
  innate capacity 28 n.7
  justice/ultimate justice 21–2, 24, 26–8, 30, 33–4
  mankind 28–9
  personhood 25 n.5
  reflections (terms for) 24, 27
  shadow (*see* shadows, Plato)
  Simile of the Cave 21–3, 30 n.8, 53
  society 21, 23, 33–4
  Sun 23–4, 27
  on Homer 136, 136 n.17
  Parmenides 38
  philosophers 21, 25–7, 33–6
  Platonic/Platonism/Platonists 41–4, 49, 55, 73–4, 76, 97–100, 104, 124
  Republic 21, 23, 25, 33 n.16, 35
Plotinus 40–1, 60 n.48, 63, 80, 99, 109 n.50, 119, 133, 138, 147
Politis, Vasili 32 n.14
Porphyry 40–1, 99
Porter, Philip G., 'Inheriting Wittgenstein's Augustine: A Grammatical Investigation of the Incarnation' 137 n.18
portraits 2 n.2. *See also* self-portraits/self-portraiture
Protestants/Protestantism 144–5

INDEX

Queneau, Raymond, *Exercices de style* 3

Radical Orthodoxy 102–3
rationalism 30, 66–7, 145
rationality 31, 31 n.12, 145–6
reality 1–4, 7, 9 n.18, 17, 22, 26–7, 30, 32, 35 n.20, 36, 38–9, 44, 49–50, 57, 73, 78, 85, 95–8, 106, 108, 114–15, 119, 122, 141–3
   divine 37–8, 76, 110, 112–13, 119–20, 124, 126, 129–30, 133–5, 139, 143
   and existence 13, 25–6
   higher/lower 32, 36, 38, 57, 110–11, 115, 119–20, 129, 136
   independent 119, 136
   new 13, 17, 96, 98
   personal 12–14
   and politicians 1–4
   and selfie 13 (*see also* selfie)
   sole 20, 22, 28, 30
   and story 16–17
   superior 115
   ultimate 25, 38, 125, 129, 136, 140
reflection 50, 113, 136
   Plato's terms of (shadow) 24
   of reality 5–7, 23–4, 32, 96, 110
   self-reflection 13
resemblance (*similitudo*) 44, 46, 49–50, 54–6, 72–5, 130–1
Romans 2 n.2
Romans (biblical) 42–3, 61, 64
Rombs, Ronnie J., *Saint Augustine and the Fall of the Soul: Beyond O'Connel and His Critics* 40 n.3

self-fashioning 3, 3 n.3, 14–15
selfie 5–6, 11–14, 18
   and myth of Echo and Narcissus 6 n.10, 11–13
   and reality 13
   short story 6, 13–14
self-loathing 82 n.33
self-portraits/self-portraiture 12, 12 n.25, 16. *See also* portraits
self-reference/self-referential character 95, 106, 108, 110, 116–27
shadows, Plato 22–7, 30–3, 141–3
   and darkness 22, 24, 26, 28, 35, 141
   Good/Evil 32 n.13, 36
   and images 35–6
   light/world of light 22–3, 25, 29, 32, 36
sin 57–69, 71, 77–8, 81, 113, 116–17, 126, 141. *See also* Adam and Eve; atonement
Socrates 21, 33, 33 n.16
   on good in daily lives 27 n.6
soteriology 97–8, 98 n.2
Stone, Greg 11
subject 9–11, 39, 93, 122. *See also* objects
   and its accident 51–2
subjectivism 122, 124
Symmachus 40

Taylor, Charles 102, 122
   Sources of the Self 122 n.78
Teske, R. J., 'The Image and Likeness of God in St. Augustine's *De Genesi* ad *Litteram Liber Imperfectus*' 90 n.45
theodicy 64 n.58, 79
thinking 1, 3, 29, 96, 114–15
   about God 38–9
   and being 96, 136

Christian 53
and memory 114 (*see also* memory/memories)
Trinity 94–100, 108 n.49, 110, 112–13, 132, 137
divine 75, 96
and human dissimilarity 53–8
truth 11, 13, 16–18, 23, 27, 30, 33–5, 35 n.20, 52, 98, 105–6, 134, 139, 144
and falsehood 46–52, 73, 75, 77, 81, 131
and mathematics 46, 51
simple 49
ultimate 43, 52

Victorinus, Marius 45 n.12, 100
Vinzent, Markus 101, 103

Wetzel, James, 'Augustine on the Will' 65 n.59

wisdom, knowledge and 23, 115, 133
words/Word 3–4, 37, 39, 41, 136–7, 143. *See also* language
of God/divine Word 74–5, 130–4, 137–9
human 74–5, 130–2
world, image and 1, 3–4, 44, 85, 110, 112, 116, 145, 147

Yin Yam, Cheuk, 'A Mind-Centered Approach of "Imago Dei": A Dynamic Construction in Augustine's De Trinitate XV' 91 n.46

Zwollo, Laela, *St Augustine and Plotinus: The Human Mind as Image of the Divine* 60 n.48

Lightning Source UK Ltd.
Milton Keynes UK
UKHW020150250122
397663UK00007B/230